Hope for the Best

Kate Cavanaugh

Other books written by Kate Cavanaugh:
MOTHER'S DAY
I CAN'T SLEEP WITH THOSE ELVES WATCHING ME
PETE'S LOST
PETE GOES TO GRAND ISLAND

Other books illustrated by KC Kiner:
I CAN'T SLEEP WITH THOSE ELVES WATCHING ME
PETE'S LOST
PETE GOES TO GRAND ISLAND

Hope for the Best

written by **KATE CAVANAUGH**
illustrated by **KC KINER**

Prairie Wind Library

KAC
inc

KAC INC.
OMAHA, NEBRASKA
1993

Printed in the United States of America

Library of Congress Catalog Card Number: 93-91474

ISBN 0-9622353-5-0

First printing November, 1993

Columns from January, 1989 to September, 1993 originally
published by *Omaha World Herald*

*This book is dedicated to the memory of my Dad, Bill Barrett, who
died at the age of 77 on September 26, 1993*

He gave me a wonderful life and the ability to always
HOPE FOR THE BEST

Bill and Evelyn Barrett dancing the night away!!

Table of Contents

Introduction

1 January

2 February

3 March

Table of Contents

Table of Contents

Table of Contents

KC AT WORK

THERE'S MORE FROM KATE!

My book is full of simple ideas that have been excessively told. I love to talk and I love to write. Luckily, I don't use as many words when I write as I do when I talk. If I did this book would be the size of a set of encyclopedias. There would be a chapter on Halloween costumes, a volume on Christmas decorations, and a second set filled with laundry and dish washing tales.

From January, 1989 to September, 1993 I have written 225 columns for The Omaha World Herald. I wanted to include all of them but I knew if I did the book would be too big or it would be necessary to read it using a magnifying glass.

I have been writing a column since 1977. I write as I think and how I see things. I tell stories about myself, my family, my friends and folks I meet and how we all get through life.

My husband, John Cavanaugh, and I have eight children. Patrick, Colleen, Maureen, Machaela, John, Michael, Peter, and Matthew, who is sometimes called Chewy. They all appear in the book regularly and fairly equally. I counted to be sure.

My parents, Bill and Evelyn Barrett, made homes in St. Charles, Illinois and at Fontana on Geneva Lake, Wisconsin. Both of these spots are frequently mentioned in my columns. My three brothers and four sisters and their families live in five different states.

John's mother, Kathleen Cavanaugh, who has provided me with material for many episodes, lives here in Omaha. John's two brothers and three sisters and their families live in Nebraska.

This large extended family provides me with plenty of story material and my children with numerous cousins and aunts and uncles.

The themes that I was happy to see reoccur in my

columns as I prepared this book for publication were:
  * the importance of unconditional love
  * life is more fun if you have an occasional crazy idea
  * be generous with your good fortune
  * it helps if you can go with the flow.

I was also impressed at all the terrific advice, wisdom and thought provoking ideas I imparted to my readers as I ended my columns.

For example:
  * Did you know if you have mice that mousetraps and peanut butter are income tax deductions?
  * It was probably for the best, isn't it always?
  * There's a lot of good things back in style from the 60's and 70's. War is not one of them.
  * I just have to remember when I get up in the morning to walk on my feet instead of my hands.
  * I think it's because I could never blow bubbles.
  * Most of these outings (pre-school field trips) have been fun and sometimes it has been just as much fun to stay home and hear about them afterward.
  * I describe myself as a naturally curious sort. My kids say the word for that is nosy.
  * Now I'm wondering how a trash bag suitcase will travel by mail.

When I'm asked if I ever run out of column ideas I say no because I get my ideas from life and it is always going on. Life comes one day at a time. The days roll into months and the months turn over into years.

While I'm living this life I think it's best to do my best and to hope for the best.

Kate Cavanaugh
October, 1993

JANUARY

January is just the month to jump with
New Year's joy, to eat no junk food, dance
the jitterbug, listen to jazz, stay out of
jail, play jeopardy, wear jade earrings, write
in a journal your plans for a June garden,
and if you have jury duty to be just.

JANUARY

Sunday	Monday	Tuesday	Wednesday	Thursday	Friday	Saturday
						1 New Year's Day
2	3	4	5	6	7	8
9	10	11	12	13 *COLLEEN'S BIRTHDAY*	14	15
16	17 Martin Luther King, Jr. Day *MACHAELA'S BIRTHDAY*	18	19	20	21	22
23 30	24 31	25	26	27	28	29

JANUARY

Decorations Come Down

Many folks take down their decorations soon after New Year's Day. I'm a hold out for tradition. Our decorations stay up through January 6th. which is the feast of the Epiphany and the 12th day of Christmas.

This is my sign that the Christmas season is over and it is time to defrock the house of red bows, greenery, lights, Santa, the reindeer and the Nativity set.

It is a relief to have the job completed, yet I feel sad. The house looked so pretty.

The Christmas tree still was fresh and could have stayed up a few more weeks. However, I wanted to spare the embarrassment of friends asking if we follow a different calendar that celebrates Christmas in February or if the tree is a Lenten ritual.

The defrocking process took a couple of days. The kitchen table was covered with ornaments, lights and other trimmings, so we had to eat either in the dining room or at the table surrounded by the remains of Christmas.

Maureen, who was eager to go shopping one day, offered to help take down the tree. She placed all the ornaments carefully on the table and began taking off the lights.

As she did her Dad entered the room. He told her to take the bulbs out of the sockets and place them individually into boxes.

"That is not how I would do it," I thought. Nor is it how I have ever done it.

My modus operandi is to put away the strings of lights with the bulbs still attached. I do this, of course, when John is not home.

I just have to make sure that I'm the one who takes the lights out of the box the next Christmas. I keep my fingers crossed that John thinks the bulbs have just been inserted as I string the lights. (Thank goodness he does not know the lights were bunched together in a box with a musical Rudolph and our Christmas stockings.)

I was still in the Christmas spirit the day Maureen removed the lights, so I didn't initiate an exchange of the pros and cons of de-bulbing or not de-bulbing the lights.

I let Maureen proceed as her Dad suggested. A problem arose when we needed to find a box for the bulbs. I couldn't find one because I threw it away several years ago when I realized I never used it.

I told Maureen and John I'd do it later and I did. I put the bulbs away in a wooden sleigh left from a floral arrangement. I hope I remember next December that I did and can find them again.

I always wonder what to do with the poinsettias. I can't throw them out; I'd feel heartless discarding something which was so beautiful and pleasurable during the holidays.

If the flowers last until February, they can be Valentine's Day decorations.

With the Christmas wreath gone, the front door looks bare, too. I think a happy home should have a door decoration, but I'm between door hangings. It's too early for a Spring wreath or a St. Patrick's Day decoration.

I think we should start a custom of keeping our outdoor Christmas decorations up through the winter. I enjoy the decorations which remain on some homes.

We wouldn't have to light the outdoor lights every night, although I like that idea, too, and have seen it done in some ski resorts.

Holiday decorations could be our flowers of the winter - just as tulips are in the spring, petunias are in the summer and mums are in the fall.

If you haven't taken down your holiday decorations, yet, don't worry because you have made me happy.

January 15, 1990

* * * *

Family's Fridge Runneth
Over With Leftovers

The salad didn't taste very good. The lettuce was limp. The tomatoes, mushrooms and cucumbers were soggy. The dressing was runny.

But I ate it anyway. I had to, in order to save face.

The evening before when Colleen was doing the dinner dishes, she asked if she could dispose of the leftover salad.

I said, "No, put it in a smaller bowl in the refrigerator. I'll have it tomorrow for lunch."

"You won't," she said. "You always say that, but you'll forget about eating it. You'll eat something else, you'll go out to lunch, someone

20 JANUARY

will bring over lunch or you won't eat at all, but it is a sure bet that you won't be eating that salad tomorrow.

"The refrigerator is filled with leftovers you are sure someone will eat but no one ever does unless Jughead comes over," she said. (Jughead is a friend who will eat anything.)

"The dishes of leftovers crowd up the refrigerator shelves making a mess until they are thrown out to make room for more leftovers."

Colleen was on a roll as she continued her lecture.

"And you always put half-filled glasses of milk in the refrigerator. Do you think there is any possibility that someone will drink leftover milk with cracker crumbs floating in it?

"The only benefit I can see in saving milk is that when the glass tips over and spills onto a leftover dish, you have to get rid of it before it is covered with mold."

Colleen is right. I do save things with great expectation for a delicious lunch or simple dinner the next day, but it doesn't work out as often as I expect.

The refrigerator is suffering right now from "leftover overload," plus it has an additional case of the "opened duplicates."

There are four one-gallon milk containers on the shelves. Three are open. One has about an inch of milk, another is half full and has a butter knife sunk in it, (don't ask me why, I don't know) and the third gallon is three-fourths full.

We have three cartons of eggnog - all open. There also is a large pitcher of water. It's there as an incentive to us to drink more water. However, it is unreachable because it is surrounded by containers.

I had planned to serve a bowl of leftover potatoes one night with some other leftovers. It was going to be a fast, slopped-together meal.

But when my brother called to say he would be in town for dinner, I decided to make a "real" meal of spaghetti.

Now we have the dish of potatoes, two leftover pork chops, six meatballs, one-half can of cranberry sauce, a saucer of salmon, a coffee cup of broccoli and a cereal bowl of spaghetti.

Other space fillers are the bottles of condiments. There are three bottles of the same brand and flavor of barbecue sauce - each with the same amount of sauce.

There also are a lot of mustard jars (but they at least are different kinds) and two pickle jars (one contains a couple of spears, the other only pickle juice).

And I have an unopened bottle of Yago Sangria that I won as a door prize at a speaking engagement in 1985.

There are jelly and jam jars, mayonnaise bottles, and such a wide assortment of salad dressings that I probably could open a salad bar. Of course, I wouldn't have any other ingredients to put on it.

Our approach to fresh produce is to buy it and eat part of it when it is fresh. Then we put what's left into the vegetable crisper and forget about it until it gets rotten and smells. Then we throw it out.

It must sound like I'm trying to be wasteful, but I'm not. I hate to see food go to waste, but the refrigerator overwhelms me.

My brother-in-law, Ken, isn't intimidated by the overflow of leftovers. At family gatherings, he rummages through the refrigerator collecting the leftovers and concocts some dish.

While he's cooking, he is subjected to a verbal barrage because he makes a mess. But we always eat what he makes and it almost always tastes good. He even washes the dishes.

All this discussion about the contents of my refrigerator has motivated me. I'm going to clean it out right now. Is anyone hungry?

January 8, 1990

* * * *

Sled Ride Was Bumpier
Than It Used to Be

It's snowing. The kids are excited because they think they might get a day off from school. I hope they have school, but I'm sort of excited about the snowfall.

Snowstorms halt a lot of plans. But if you don't have anywhere to go, have heat in the house and chocolate chip cookie fixings in the pantry, a snowy day can be therapeutic.

This winter, it seems we have had a lot of the right kind of snow. You know, the snow that's good for sledding.

Another good kind of snow is the type that's good packing snow for making a snowman.

Behind our house there's a park with a great sledding hill. The kids always run over there to sled as soon as there's a light covering of snow.

I hadn't been over there to sled in years, but over the holidays, all the guys were going and I decided I'd join the fun.

I looked so well-padded when I bundled up that I hoped I wouldn't see any neighbors. I feared my quilted snow pants would cause me to be mistaken for Tommy LaSorda before his Ultra Slimfast diet.

When I arrived at the park, there was an assortment of sleds. Going down the hill on one of the saucers appealed to me the most, but it was taken, so I chose to go on a sled that is made of thin plastic and rolls up into a cylinder when not in use.

The snow looked very soft and fluffy, and I was very well-padded by flesh and by fabric, but none of the cushioning was any match for the earth beneath me.

Solid ground was exactly that - and it seemed even harder when I was gliding over it on the plastic magic carpet misrepresenting itself as a sled.

After that first run down the hill - when each ripple on the terrain went directly from my posterior through my interior and out to my exterior - I concluded that unless I wanted to exchange the sled for a chiropractor's bed, I better do my sleigh-riding on a more deluxe sleigh - or at least something with a little more surface between me and Mother Nature's lap.

I went back to the house for the old toboggan. It's warped, and I figured we might not be able to get up much momentum on the sledding hill, but I piled a couple of the guys on and started pushing it off.

It wouldn't budge. So, I worked on it from the front. No luck. Finally, I was able to get it going when we hit some ice. We slid down the hill sideways and backward. It was fun - I think.

Getting back up the hill was tricky. I had Matt, who kept slipping on the ice, under one arm, and the toboggan under the other.

A few days and several inches of new snow later, I walked Matt over to the hill to join his siblings. This time, I hadn't planned to stay. But I did.

It was dark and the moonlight (actually it was a street light) shining on the snowy hill put me in a reminiscing mood.

When Johnny took me to the other side of the park so I could take a more gentle run across the park, I started remembering all the tobogganing and sledding outings at Pottawattamie Park on the golf course in St. Charles, Illinois. We'd fly over the sandtraps, lean left or right on the toboggan to avoid the trees or aim the sled to glide straight through the clump of evergreen trees and finally stop just short of sailing into the Fox River. It was fun and exciting to do then and to remember now. But, boy, am I glad that's in the past.

I wonder when I lost my nerve? It probably went out with my back on that last run.

January 15, 1991

* * * *

War Casts Shadow
Over Family Activities

"Am I going to always remember what I was doing at 5:40 p.m., January 16, 1991, like you and Dad can remember where you were when President Kennedy was shot and my grandparents can recreate in their minds December 7, 1941?" Colleen asked me late on the evening of January 16.

"I hope not," I answered, because the events on December 7, 1941, dramatically affected the world as Colleen's grandparents knew it and the tragedy on November 22, 1963, marked the end of an era of fabulous expectation for the future of my generation.

But I'm afraid Colleen - and everyone else - will remember January 16 as the day America went to war.

Maybe, by the time this column is in print, the war will be over, our troops will be making plans to return home, and the terms of peace will be the new words in our vocabulary instead of terrifying and ominous words such as scud missile and sorties.

Maybe our evenings once again will be spent with Johnny Carson, Jay Leno, and David Letterman instead of Tom Brokaw, Peter Jennings and CNN journalists wearing gas masks, because the only glimpse of war found anywhere will be from reruns of "M*A*S*H."

"How did this happen?" my teen-age daughter asked. "Last year, we were so excited because world peace seemed like a genuine possibility. The Berlin Wall was down and the prospects for improving relations with Eastern Europe were up. Now we're into this. What a mess!"

Everything is affected by war. My family has celebrated two birthdays this past week. Colleen's took place on the weekend when

Congress was debating resolutions of war. Her celebration was dampened by this discussion.

Machaela had a party planned for her birthday. The celebration began just as we heard that Israel was being attacked.

To keep the little guys out of the way during her party, Machaela wanted me to get a movie for them to watch on the videocassette recorder. While we were in the video store, I felt like someone who would spend Good Friday afternoon in a pool hall. Picking out a movie didn't seem like the appropriate thing to do at such a time.

We are doing all the usual things, but big black clouds created by the Desert Storm loom overhead, blocking the sunshine. We are very frightened for the members of our armed forces and the innocent people of Israel and the Middle East. We're worried about the future.

We've been reminiscing about the Vietnam era. Colleen wanted to know how old I was when it all began - I was about her age, a high school girl. By the time it was over, I had graduated from college, taught school, been married and was the mother of two children. Colleen was a baby. After we figured that out, both of us got a chilly feeling.

During the Vietnam War, there was constant uncertainty about the future, but the young people still moved forward in life. We went to school, laughed, danced wild, lived it up too much. Some of us even got jobs. The girls shortened their skirts and the guys grew their hair long, if they weren't in the military service.

Then there were the weddings, followed by baby showers and babies. We hung wallpaper in our kitchens and paid the bills. There was also an ongoing discussion about our country's policy. And overshadowing it all the time was the fear and concern for everyone in harm's way.

I want my children to have all the good experiences my generation had, but I don't want these experiences shaped by the experience of war.

The direction of our lives then was decided by draft status and lottery numbers and leave time and military orders.

I am a woman and was not required to serve, but when you have a brother, husband and friends in the middle of it all, you are serving your country. Just as the families of all our troops involved in Desert Shield are serving.

President Bush has promised that the war in the Persian Gulf will not be another Vietnam. I hope and pray that he will be able to keep that promise.

There's a lot of good things back in style from the '60s and early '70s but war is not one of them.

January 22, 1991

* * * *

Experience Helped To Get Around D.C.

The last inauguration I attended was that of Jimmy Carter in 1977. My husband, John, was a freshman congressman from Nebraska. We had been living in Washington, D.C., for only two weeks, so we didn't know our way around. Nevertheless, it was an exciting experience.

John and I have just returned from attending the inaugural festivities in Washington, D.C., for President Clinton and Vice President Gore. John is no longer in Congress. We no longer live in Washington, D.C. Now we know our way around the city. And once more it was an exciting experience.

One difference in this inauguration from the one in 1977 is that the Metro, the subway, now is in full operation. In 1977 only a short span was operating.

I love taking the Metro when I'm in Washington. It is clean, fast and efficient. John and I thought it would be a good idea to take it on Inauguration Day from Foggy Bottom, the stop by our hotel, to the Capitol South stop by the Capitol to attend the swearing-in ceremonies.

Several other people had the same idea. The Washington Post reported that 406,117 people rode the Metro that day compared with 250,000 on an average weekday. According to the District of Columbia police, an estimated 800,000 people were in attendance in downtown Washington to watch either the swearing-in ceremony at the Capitol or the parade on Pennsylvania Avenue.

The subway platform at Foggy Bottom was crowded but manageable. But when the train arrived it was already almost full. When we stepped aboard I thought the riders would move farther in, but there was no place for them to go. Just as the doors began to close, John was nudged backward and off the train. We were holding hands so his arm was still aboard. I couldn't get off and I was afraid John would be dragged alongside the train. I quickly let go of his hand and he was able to pull his arm out, the doors closed and off I went.

I thought John would take the next train and we'd meet at the Capitol South stop. However, our train didn't stop there because the platform was too crowded to accommodate the passengers.

I got off at the next stop, where I ran into Rep. Peter Hoagland, D-Neb., with his son Nicholas, 2, in his arms and his son David, 8, at his side. He, too, had been separated at the Metro stop from his wife, Barbara, and their three other children. I told Peter I would help him with the children.

We waited for the next train to come to see if John was on it, but it arrived almost empty because unlike what happened on our train, it was announced to those passengers to get off at Federal Center Southwest, the stop before Capitol South, which is much closer to the Capitol than where we had ended up. I figured that's where John would be.

So Peter, the children and I took the next train back to Federal Center Southwest. Peter spotted John among the throng of people. An advantage of being more than 6 feet tall, as are both Peter and John, is seeing and being seen in a crowd. We learned later that Barbara and the other children managed fine.

It was an exhilarating day. The crowds, which were remarkably patient and enthusiastic, added to the gaiety of the occasion. And the weather was magnificent.

In this situation it helped to have some familiarity of the city. John and I reminisced about Carter's inaugural. That year, we got separated after the ceremonies en route to a parade-watching party. Our children, who were very young, were with me and my sister, Mary Pat. I thought we were pretty resourceful. Mary Pat flagged down a bus that was shuttling people back across the Potomac River to their cars to give us a ride at least part way to our destination.

John remembers spending Inauguration Day 1977 frantically searching the parade route for his family. We didn't want to repeat that experience in 1993. After the Metro ride in the morning, we made sure we were inseparable the rest of the day.

January 26, 1993

* * * *

 JANUARY

Senior Photo Sitting Presents A Time of Memories, Choices

Colleen, my oldest daughter, will graduate high school in May. Of course, it seems like only yesterday that I was taking her to the photographer to have her first baby picture taken. I bathed her and made a finger curl in her hair. I dressed her in a pink dress with accordion pleats down the front, puffed sleeves and a lace collar. While the picture was being taken I had to hover in the background in case she tipped over because she was propped up against a blanket covered box.

But, oh my, she was gorgeous. I love the feeling of that picture. It showed delicate and natural beauty. We bought the whole set. After all, she was only going to be a baby once, right?

We've had 18 years full of yesterdays since then, and now we're involved in the senior picture session. Colleen is still gorgeous, I'm still hovering in the background of her life (much to her chagrin) just in case she tips over, and my ideas for her portrait are the same.

Remember when a graduation picture was a head shot with the senior wearing a cashmere or a cashmere-clone sweater? Well, times have changed. That's OK. I told Colleen to go for it, to get the picture done the way it's done these days. And she did.

She tells me her photography session that included two changes of clothes, eight poses and only two different backgrounds was considerably less involved than some seniors. Those classmates changed clothes four times, traveled around town scouting backgrounds and brought in props for the photograph such as their car, horse, dog, trombone, leather jacket or best friend.

The result of Colleen's session was two foldout proof books for us to look over and to make our selection. In order to bring these proofs home we had to put down a sizable deposit that would either be refunded or applied to our order.

The only benefit to this was by the time it came to ordering the finished pictures I had already written off the deposit as used up money and spent a lot more money without realizing the grand total.

Everyone had a favorite pose of Colleen to be made up in our choice of either the expensive finish, the even more expensive finish, or the absolutely, unbelievably most expensive finish, except Colleen's dad. When we sat down to choose what we wanted after a month of poring over and discussing what pose to get, he said the same thing he said the day Colleen brought the proofs home, "I like all of them. Can't we get all of them?"

"No, we can't," I told him thinking to myself. "Not if we want to continue buying groceries."

I don't think he made the association that the 1990s pictures came with 1990s prices.

It was hard to decide what proof to have made into the finished portrait. There were poses of her head and shoulders, of her sitting on the floor hugging her knee in one outfit and hugging her other knee in the other outfit. There was the pose of her standing in ballet's third position and one kneeling like she was about to jump up and run off.

In the poses I liked, Colleen didn't like because of the way her hair looked. "It reminds me of a '70s prom queen," she said. In the ones she liked I didn't like her expression. I wanted smiley, she wanted sensuous. I liked the cute ones, she thought they were cheesy. I leaned toward the innocent pose, she said she looked ill.

Finally, we did what her Dad suggested. We bought almost all of the pictures. After all you only graduate from high school once. Isn't that right?

January 28, 1992

* * * *

'Friend' Is Tuckered Out From All That Nitpicking

This tale is guaranteed to have you scratching your head.

It's a true story which has been fictionalized to protect the innocent - meaning me. So I'll tell you about what happened to a "friend" I know.

"We had lice at our house over the weekend," she said. "Have you ever had head lice?

"It's a big pain in the scalp. This is what happened . . ."

She said some friends had stopped by. While they were visiting, their daughter's itchy scalp came up in the conversation.

Another friend - who has medical training - had looked at the

child's head and diagnosed head lice.

The mother promptly telephoned the doctor to find out what to do and proceeded to take care of the problem.

"Well," the woman continued, "I felt bad for my friend, especially when she telephoned me later to tell me that one of her other children also had lice. And she described everything she had to do to get rid of them.

"But then I got busy and didn't think about it again until a few days later when I was shopping with one of my daughters. I looked down at her head and noticed white flakes.

"At first, I thought it was dandruff, but the flakes looked awfully similar to those on her friend's head. My daughter then reminded me that she had slept at her friend's house the weekend before.

"It had to be lice. I called the doctor to get a prescription for Kwell, a shampoo used to treat head lice.

"The next step was to begin the ritual of checking all the other heads in the house. Everyone else appeared to be free of lice.

"I had to shampoo only one head, but it was difficult. Even though the infestation was small and hard to see, all of her hair had to be thoroughly shampooed, and she has long, thick hair.

"We washed it in the kitchen sink. I wore rubber gloves. While I was shampooing, I remembered a scene from the book, 'Thornbirds,' in which the protagonist, who has long, beautiful hair, comes home from school with lice. Her parents cut her hair at the scalp to get rid of the lice. They must not have heard of Kwell.

"My next stop was another trip to the pharmacy for a lice comb. After the hair is shampooed, it must be combed with a special comb to get out the nits, which are louse eggs. That must be where the term nitpicking originated.

"The pharmacist gave me a fact sheet on head lice. I posted it in the kitchen and have read it so often that I can now recite from it.

"After the shampooing was completed, we called our neighbors and friends with the good news that they also might get lice, and then we set about delousing the house.

"I issued an all-points bulletin for bedding, coats, hats, scarfs, headbands, barrettes and stuffed animals. The washer and dryer began a marathon workout.

"The things I didn't want to wash or dry were put in a trash bag and sealed for 10 days. With determination, we vacuumed all the furniture and rugs.

"The head lice fact sheet indicated there is a spray to use on furniture, but it's not necessary. I hope that's true.

"I tried to keep people's heads off the sofa and the car seat, but it was hopeless. So I kept checking heads for my next case. I figured it was inevitable that we'd have at least one more victim."

"We did, and of course it had to be the child with so much hair that in comparison, Lady Godiva looks like she just finished Army boot camp.

"The whole production of washing, drying and vacuuming was repeated, but this time it was done with a lot less enthusiasm.

"After that I washed my own hair with the hottest water I could stand. I figured if lice were planning to set up residence in my hair, I wanted to give them a warm welcome.

"I've given up combing and brushing my hair. Even though we've deloused all the brushes and combs, I'm not taking any chances. I'd rather look messy."

"Gee," I told my "friend." "Your experience sounds awful."

"Oh, no," she said with exaggerated denial, "it was great fun - so much so that we are hoping to discover a couple cases of athlete's foot next weekend."

January 29, 1990

* * * *

FEBRUARY

February finishes the winter birthdays. To feed a fever or to fire up feelings in an old flame eat a few chocolates on the fourteenth. To say "I love you forever" bring fresh flowers from a florist, then make fondue and do a folk dance by the fireplace or take a far flung trip in a flying machine.

FEBRUARY

Sunday	Monday	Tuesday	Wednesday	Thursday	Friday	Saturday
		1 *MIKE'S BIRTHDAY*	2 Groundhog Day	3	4	5
6	7	8	9	10	11	12
13	14 Valentine's Day	15	16 Ash Wednesday	17	18	19
20	21 Presidents' Day	22	23	24	25	26
27	28					

FEBRUARY

Kids' Grammar Gives Mom the Heebie-Jeebies

"Me and Andrea are going to the movies," Colleen announced.

"No, 'Andrea and I are going,' " I said.

"You and Andrea are going?" Colleen asked in puzzlement.

"No, I'm not going. I was correcting what you said."

"What's wrong with what I said?" "You know what I mean."

"When speaking about yourself and another person, put the other person's name ahead of yours."

"What difference does it make?" Colleen persisted.

"It bothers me. It is not correct grammar, and I don't like the way it sounds, OK? When you are speaking, be humble and think of the other person as someone important whose name should be given prominence over yours."

"What if he's a sleaze? What if we just committed a crime together and it was all his idea? Would it still be correct to say, 'The big creep and I just held up a liquor store'?" Colleen asked.

"Well, in that situation you can make an exception and say, 'me and the big creep,' but I'd rather you never have that kind of news to report. If you did, you could end up in a place that would have a terrible influence on your speech."

My kids think I'm a nerd when I correct their grammar. I tell them that if they go through life speaking incorrectly, they will be nerds.

Maureen disagrees with my logic.

Whenever she says, "Tell him to do it hisself," I get the heebie-jeebies.

"It's himself; hisself is not a word," I tell her. "Speaking like that has the same effect on your listeners' ears as hearing a speaker burp in the middle of a dignified speech."

"So what? When I'm a famous fashion designer no one will care if I make up my own pronouns or use the ones from a language book, or for that matter, burp while I'm talking."

Although, I react to my children's grammar as if I know it all, I am not a linguist. Correct usage of pronouns has pretty well sunk into my memory, as has the usage of most verbs.

I know when to use "do" and "does," and "was" and "were."

I know not to dangle my participles or split my infinitives, although, I probably do both on occasion.

Some things, however, never seem to sink in. When I inquire

about someone's health, should I say: "Aren't you feeling well?" or "Aren't you feeling good?"

I know one word describes well-being and the other refers to one's ability to feel things.

I never can remember which is which, so I solve the problem by rearranging the question: "How is your health?" or "How's your sense of touch?"

Those lie and lay words always are laying for me. If I think about it, I know that you "lay" the book on the table and that you "lie" on the couch, but I'm a fast talker and I don't have time to decline verbs before I use them.

Oftentimes, even if I am aware of the correct word form, the incorrect form slips out before I get a chance to apprehend it.

Maybe I should review the verb "to lie" right now so I will get it right the next time.

Here goes: The present tense of lie is lie; I lie in bed. The past tense is lay; I lay in bed yesterday. The future perfect tense is lain; tomorrow I will have lain in bed for three days.

But what about the present participle? Is it laying or lying? It's lying. If I were laying, to be grammatically correct, I better be putting down something other than myself.

I think all of these verb forms are correct; but if they are not, you will know I am lying - you will know I am not telling the truth.

February 6, 1989

* * * *

2 Stuffed Cats Help Siblings Relive Closeness

My brother, Peter, lives in the San Francisco Bay area so I don't see him very often. Occasionally, he goes to Illinois and Wisconsin for summer family reunions and for holidays. And once in a while he makes the trip to Omaha.

We always are happy to have Peter visit. The kids really have a good time listening to his crazy stories. He gathers the kids around the television, turns down the sound and creates his own version of what is happening on the screen.

Peter is an artist and cartoonist and operates his own T-shirt business. He manages to get by. He is not married and has no children. Peter is very independent.

We were born only 14 months apart, but our lives could not be more different. As a wife and mother, I live a life rooted to a commitment of meeting the needs of others.

I love it that way and can't imagine living any other way. My life is fulfilling and filled with love. It is the route I have chosen, and I am happy with it.

My brother has none of these trappings nor the physical comforts I require, and he wants it that way. He is happy, with a life filled with friends, his work and bicycling all over the beautiful countryside where he lives.

My husband, John, had some business in San Francisco recently, and I went along for a few days. While in San Francisco, we visited Peter.

I wanted to see where he lives, hangs out and works. I wanted to meet his friends. So, after so many years of visualizing what his life must be like, I finally got to see it for myself.

Everything was pretty much as I expected. His place could be described as a "no-frills" environment with a spectacular view of the scenery.

When Peter noticed the look on my face as I surveyed his digs - and knowing my eye for orderliness - he said, "Out here it doesn't matter how you live because you always are outdoors."

After observing all the grand homes in the area, I doubted that everyone agreed with that notion, but in Peter's case it applies and that is what's important.

I discovered the Kitty Mertz sitting on top of the windowsill in Peter's bedroom. I was so delighted to see them. The Kitty Mertz are Peter's two stuffed black cats that he has had since the early 1950s.

Peter received them as Christmas gifts from Aunt Clara. He got one stuffed cat one year and the other cat the following year. Their names are Ricky and Micky Mertz. They are named for Fred and Ethel Mertz, Lucy and Ricky Ricardo's neighbors on the "I Love Lucy" show.

Peter took down the Kitty Mertz from the windowsill so I could hug them. John took some pictures of Peter, me and the Mertz boys. Peter posed with one of the Mertzes on each of his shoulders with the kitties' arms around his neck.

We reminisced over the Mertzes' lives.

Grandma Hardt, who lived with us, always repaired the Mertzes as their appendages came loose. Once a year she would sew new suits from the remnants of flannel material that she had used to make pajamas for us.

That brought back memories, too. One of the Kitty Mertz was left behind in a motel where our family stayed on vacation.

Peter was heartbroken, but things brightened up when the kitty arrived by mail a few day later. A manager at the hotel found the kitty under a bed and mailed it to our house.

Seeing the Kitty Mertz again after so many years really affected me. The stuffed animals are symbols of the closeness siblings have when they are raised together.

No matter what happens, that closeness always is there.

The feeling sometimes has to be resurrected like a long-lost stuffed toy, but once unearthed and dusted off, you can embrace the feeling as if yesteryear were only yesterday.

I would have been content just to have seen Peter again, but finding the Mertzes created an intersection where the past and present of two different roads of life met.

I liked that.

February 12, 1990

* * * *

Mom Likes Job At the Library

My volunteer job this year at St. Joan of Arc School, where some of my children attend, is helping librarian Carol Nish. My motives for library duty are not entirely unselfish because I chose to help with Pete's second-grade class and Matt's kindergarten class.

The boys like to have me there, but they don't think I contribute much to the workings of the library. Pete once commented, "You don't do much in the library. You are always reading." My first thought was to reply, "Well, isn't that what you are supposed to do in the library?"

He is correct. I am reading. I have fun reading parts of books as I put them back on the shelf. I read an excerpt from a book on the Kennedys in which Mrs. Kennedy's maid described Jackie's ritual of eating breakfast in bed. I also read a book on learning to scuba dive in a swimming pool.

I enjoy reading children's books. While checking-in returned books, I frequently see a couple of interesting books that I rapidly read. When I'm putting the books on the shelves I usually come across one that I pull out to read. Sometimes the reading slows down the book shelving, but I can't resist browsing.

When the children bring their books to check out, I go through the book to see if it looks interesting. It appears that children go through phases of interest. For a few weeks several second-graders were checking out the "101 Jokes" books. And a book on insects was really popular recently with the kindergarten boys.

Lately Pete has checked out the Time Machine Books, which are time-traveling stories that allow you to choose your own adventure. He has his dad involved with him in this reading escapade.

I can usually talk Matt into checking out a book that I've found but didn't have time to read. Last week he took out Jan Brett's "Berlioz," which is a story about a bear's orchestra. Jan Brett's illustrations are beautifully detailed. I wanted to have the book at home so I could spend more time reading it.

One day I read "If You Give a Moose a Muffin," written by Laura Joffe Numeroff and illustrated by Felicia Bond. I enjoyed it immensely, but my hearty laughs were beginning to be embarrassing. I checked out the book so I could yuk it up privately at home.

Another fun book was "The Principal's New Clothes," written by Stephanie Calmenson and illustrated by Denise Brunkus. The book jacket describes it as a hilarious, updated version of the famous Hans Christian Anderson fairy tale.

The book has been nominated for a Golden Sower Award, which is given in Nebraska each year for children's literature. Nebraska elementary-school students read from the selections on the list of nominees and vote for their favorite books.

I enjoy listening to the stories Mrs. Nish reads to the children as I put away the books. I'm not the only parent volunteer who enjoys listening. Bernie Irvine told me she helps out every other week for the fourth-graders, who have a novel read to them. She always asks Mrs. Nish, "What happened last week when I wasn't here?"

The students learn to use the resources libraries make available to

FEBRUARY

them. Mrs. Nish says her goal is for the students to feel comfortable using a library and to continue using it throughout their lives. If they do, library time will be a time for all, all the time.

February 16, 1993

* * * *

These 'Fathers' Come in Handy As Baby Sitters

When I mention that I've been on a trip, the question I'm often asked is not, "Did you have a good time?" but "Who takes care of the children while you're gone?"

That's a good question.

Although, I don't go away from home without the children very often, when I do it requires some strategic planning.

Sometimes this arrangement-making is so involved that I wonder if the getaway is worth it. (I always decide it is once I'm out of here.)

Recently, I had such an opportunity - and we had some prestigious baby sitters riding herd back at the ranch. They were the Reverends. Timothy Lannon, president of Creighton Prep, and Terry Brennan, a teacher at Prep.

How did we swing that? Answer: BASH. Last spring, John and I attended BASH - which stands for Building a Scholastic Heritage. It is a Creighton Prep fund-raising dinner and auction.

One of the items on the auction block was weekend baby-sitting services by Father Lannon and Father Brennan.

As a committee member working on BASH, I had a lot of fun speculating with the other workers who we thought should bid on this service.

It soon became a consensus that the Cavanaughs should buy it. I agreed it would be fun, but I didn't seriously consider bidding until the evening of BASH when Father Lannon stopped by our table.

"I think I'll bid on your baby-sitting services during the oral auction," I told him, somewhat in jest.

"You do?" he answered, looking a bit terrified."I think you should let someone else have it."

That clinched it! Father Lannon was afraid to come to our house

to baby-sit. I decided the only way to arrest his fears was to make him face them. After all, he's from a big family and should be able to manage.

I won the bid.

What did he expect when he offered his services? Did he think someone with an immaculate home and no children was going to bid so "the Fathers" could come over and baby-sit the goldfish?

That wasn't likely to happen. A realistic expectation would have been a bidder such as myself, a mother with a pack of kids, who goes out to the highways and byways in search of just such an escape.

After the shock wore off, Father Lannon resigned himself to his fate. He was determined to live up to his obligation.

Whenever John and I would see him, he would ask when we would be needing him. With BASH of 1990 fast approaching, we thought, why not?

"The Fathers" spent a weekend at our house while John and I spent a weekend away. From all reports, it wasn't as bad as they thought it might be.

I left the house loaded with food, and money to order pizza. Sunday morning, Grandma Cavanaugh arrived with doughnuts and fruit salad.

I wrote the instructions on who went where, when, and how. Most important of all, I arranged to have my college helper, Colleen Campbell, on hand to help run the show - or at least the washing machine, which is always running.

"Everything went very well," Father Lannon said upon our arrival home. "In fact, the kids were well-behaved!" (I guess there was only one altercation. Chewy bit Pete.)

He continued, "I enjoyed playing Scrabble, checkers, Solarquest and Nintendo. I felt like I was 8 years old again. I'll be over soon for Saturday morning cartoons."

The kids had fun, too.

"It was great going on field trips and playing games with 'the Fathers,' " they said, "but the best part was we didn't have to go to church. Father Lannon said Mass right here in the house - and it was a lot shorter than at church."

February 19, 1990

* * * *

Vacuum Cleaner Aggravates 'Simple' Chore

There are lots of things that can bring tears to a person's eyes. A vacuum cleaner shouldn't be one of them. But my vacuum cleaner has caused my tears to overflow. It's not an emotional response. It's one of sheer frustration.

A few years ago, I purchased a vacuum cleaner that was supposed to be a good machine, top of the line, a deluxe model. It appeared to have the ability to do its job thoroughly, powerfully, continually and easily.

All these benefits came with a hefty price tag, but it was one I was prepared to pay. There was a job to be done - cleaning my house - and this upright vacuum cleaner claimed to be up to doing it. I was excited.

But it was not to be. Operating this vacuum cleaner tops my list of aggravations.

Let's set a scene. You and I are going to clean up identical messes in our family rooms after our children's sleep-over parties. I know the children should be doing it, but just for the sake of example, let's pretend you and I are tackling the tasks. I'm at my house and you are at your house.

First, we'll put all the cushions back on the couch, fold all the blankets and pick up the pillows. Then we'll collect the pizza boxes, empty the remains of the pop cans, rewind the videotapes on the recorder, wipe all the sticky stuff off the coffee table, pick up the candy wrappers and spilled popcorn, line up all the shoes and make a pile of the dirty clothes.

Barring the necessity of cleaning up a catastrophe such as fingernail polish on the sofa or tangled mini-blinds, the clean-up task shouldn't take longer than 10 minutes to 15 minutes - until we are ready to vacuum our floors.

Vacuuming has such a wonderful cleansing effect. After all those other jobs are completed, a good go-around with the vacuum would cap off the job to perfection.

So, what happens next? We both go to our respective closets to drag out our vacuum cleaners. You plug yours in and have as much fun as you would on the dance floor as you fox-trot around your family room picking up all the debris. Before Lawrence Welk could say "ah-one," you are finished and sitting on the couch eating leftover pizza.

However, if this scene had a split screen, the half showing my

FEBRUARY

house would depict something different.

I set to work with great expectations. After a few sweeps across the floor, I realize not much is coming up. I empty the bag, heeding the advice of my mother, a champion vacuumer, that the vacuum needs air to circulate in order to operate.

I try vacuuming again - with no luck. I turn the vacuum cleaner over and discover the problem. The fan belt has fallen off again.

I have queried several friends to see if any of them have fan belt problems with their vacuum cleaners. None have. Yet the purchase and installation of fan belts are regular parts of my routine - as are repairs to the wheels, the motor, the springs and the brush. Mine is a well-maintained, ne'er-do-well vacuum cleaner.

To insert a fan belt, I once would have had to pry off the metal piece located on the vacuum cleaner's bottom. Now the metal piece practically falls off, it has been removed so often. (It also falls off while I'm vacuuming - another feature of this deluxe machine.)

Now comes the tricky part. There's a special fan-belt installing tool. I guard it like an overprotective mother hen, because without the tool it is absolutely impossible to get the fan belt attached.

With the tool, attaching the fan belt still takes a combination of fine motor skills and brute strength.

This usually is the time when the tears start. I wait until I finally get my vacuum cleaner operating before I start swearing. The noise muffles my swearing.

February 19, 1991

* * * *

'Invincible' Son Is Convinced He's Superboy

Five super boys live at our house, but one thinks he's Superboy.

That's right. My beautiful baby, Matthew, who at age 3 is not a baby anymore, thinks he's Superboy.

This is fine most of the time, except when he climbs to a high place and announces that he intends to "fly."

Matthew has few fears, other than kryptonite and making sure he gets his share of Thunder Jets candy.

Superboy has a plastic ring, which apparently contains kryptonite.

Whenever Matthew wears the ring, he talks of "getting weaker."

In order to be Superboy, my son says he has to dress like Superboy, which he does day and night. This is easy because his Superboy suits double as pajamas.

We have several sets of Superboy pj's. Grandma gave each of the little guys a pair (complete with capes) for Christmas.

The boys wore them until Matthew became invincible. Now he has full ownership of all sets of Superboy pajamas, and I don't think anyone could convince him otherwise.

The different sizes don't matter. I just roll the cuffs and sleeves for perfect fits.

The capes were attached to the pj's with Velcro tabs, but after daily washings the tabs shriveled and the capes no longer stayed in place.

This caused in-flight difficulty for Superboy: Whenever a cape slipped off, he fell from the sky - or at least that is what he said happened.

This frustrated me as well because I always was called upon to fix the capes. When Superboy flies around the house faster than a speeding bullet and leaps from tall furniture with a single bound, he tends to lose his cape a lot.

I ran into another problem one day when I couldn't find a cape to go with Superboy's shirt.

I tried to convince my son that a red Spiderman cape would be a good substitute, but it didn't work.

After that incident, I attached the Superman capes to the matching shirts with safety pins. That worked until Superboy decided the pins didn't look right.

"Superboy doesn't have pins," Matthew said. So I sewed the capes to the shirts.

Superboy does have some restrictions. For example, he only can be Superboy at home. After all, his pajamas are his uniform.

The only time Matthew strays from the crime-fighting life of Superboy is when he accidentally pulls out his Ghostbusters underwear. Then he remembers there are ghosts to bust.

He puts on his Ghostbuster suit (pajamas), pulls on his Ghostbuster backpack, grabs his Ghostbuster trap and goes to work. He says he's Peter Vinkman.

He's a Ghostbuster until he has captured all the ghosts in the house or runs into Ghostbuster slime. Then it's time to be Superboy again.

This means a complete change of clothes because Superboy never would wear Ghostbuster underwear.

Sometimes, as a compromise, I talk Superboy into wearing regular clothes over his Superboy suit. I tell him he can be Clark Kent for a while. He'll agree to this, but he still likes to leave his cape hanging out.

We try to use all of Superboy's good qualities to influence Matthew's behavior. When he bosses me around or doesn't stay in bed at night, I tell him Superboy wouldn't treat his mom that way. He tells me Superboy doesn't have a mom.

The moral to this story: Superboy makes a lot of laundry, but he also is a lot of fun.

February 26, 1990

* * * *

POPCORN

MARCH

March is the month of melting snow unless you go to the mountains. March's meatless meals mean no midnight morsels unless it's a mackerel. March's most momentous day is marked on the melodious seventeenth, the feast of the missionary, St. Patrick. A miserable mood meanders away with the arrival of buds on the magnolia tree.

MARCH

Sunday	Monday	Tuesday	Wednesday	Thursday	Friday	Saturday
		1	2	3	4	5
6	7	8	9	10	11	12
13	14	15	16	17 St. Patrick's Day	18	19
20	21	22	23	24	25	26
27 Passover Begins Palm Sunday	28	29	30	31		

MARCH

Family's Trip to Video Store Rates a 'PG'

The requests start as soon as they get home from school on Friday afternoon. First, my family wants to establish whose turn it is to have an overnight guest.

Once they've figured out who can come over, the next step is to get me to the grocery store. A Friday night needs a big dose of junk food and a video rental to be successful.

The weekend ritual of renting a movie starts out with the begging to get a movie. This is followed by my acquiescence and the trip to the video store, where the disputes begin over what to get. Someone usually ends up pouting because his or her choice wasn't picked.

Back home, hand-to-hand combat commences over who gets to be in the room to watch the movie. The ritual ends Sunday when we forget to take the movie back.

Frequently, I have my older children take my younger children to the video store. I don't need to worry about them choosing something inappropriate because Pete, who is 8, has all the ratings memorized. The other family members think he is too conscientious because he walks around the video store vetoing all his brothers' selections. "That one's R-rated," he'll say. "Mom won't let us get it."

One of my older kids is annoyed because there's a block on her name that restricts her from renting any R-rated movies. I told her I didn't remember putting it there, but as long it's there I think it is meant to be.

I like to stick to the G- or PG- rated movies. My kids describe PG movies as having only a little kissing, no one gets killed and there's no bad words.

If I do go along to the video store, I'll spend a long time trying to find something I might like to watch. When I miss seeing a movie in the theater, I plan to see it on video. But I can never remember what that movie was. If I do remember, all the copies are already checked out. Usually, what I do get doesn't matter because I ordinarily don't get around to watching it until it's time to take it back.

Sometimes when we are in the video store, my sons try to convince me that a particular movie is rated R only because of one or two bad scenes. They promise to close their eyes during those scenes.

I don't go for that idea, because in contrast to their mom's home video watching, they always watch the movies that we rent over and over. Sometimes by the time the weekend is over, the dialogue from the movie has become the dialogue of our family. So I'd need a bleeper for every other word uttered if we talked like they do in some R-rated movies.

One thing that would cause me to talk like they do in the movies (if I were a swearing woman) is late fees for overdue movies.

Several family members can travel past the video store three times the day it is due and we will all forget to return the movie. Usually we remember when we're dressed in our pajamas. One time I didn't get around to watching a two-hour movie until after 10 p.m. It was due back at midnight. I figured if we pushed fast forward on the VCR over spots that didn't seem critical to the plot, it would be over before the movie turned into a pumpkin. I thought we had made it back to the video store in time, but the next time we went to check out a movie we had a late fee.

The scene that day at the checkout could have been rated R for violence and rough language but instead I used parental guidance and caused a PG scene. I paid the fine.

March 2, 1993

* * * *

Plenty of Bear Hugs
to Go Around in This Family

Matthew has become a family man. For Christmas, our 4-year-old son's Godmother gave him a large teddy bear.

It is supposed to be a Christmas bear because he's outfitted in a red-and-green plaid sweater vest, bow tie, and floppy hat. But Matt and his brothers think the bear is dressed for golf.

Sometimes Matt dresses his bear for the beach with shorts and a T-shirt.

The bear has become a member of our family. For many years, I thought the most stressful thing in my day was finding shoes and outerwear for two toddlers and a baby. Dressing them for a ride in the car was an experience that could fulfill the endurance and physical-strength requirements necessary for an Olympic event.

I thought those days were behind me, now that I have only one child home during school hours. But the bear must go everywhere with us, and according to his pal, Matt, the bear is very sensitive to the weather. In addition to his golf outfit, he must wear socks, shoes, coat, hat and mittens. And in the car, the bear must be buckled up in a seat belt.

When we get to our destination, the bear must go inside with us because he might cry or become frightened if he's left in the car.

Matt says his bear likes the french fries from McDonald's drive-up window, but he would like to go inside sometime to see what it looks like. Matt says his bear thinks McDonald's is just a picture with a window in it where the food is delivered. Matt says he would like to go inside sometime, too.

When Matt received the bear, I didn't know there already was a bear family. His relatives include Twins, Baby Panda, Love Heart and Wrestler.

I'm happy for the bear. It's always nice to be reunited with relatives. Before this bear arrived, the bear family lived separately throughout our house. I don't think two of them even realized they were twins until Matt and his new bear explained that to them.

Now they all live on Matt's bed. He would like to take all the bears along when we go out because he thinks the bears need a baby sitter if we leave them home.

But even Matt has been overwhelmed by the large bear family. He can carry all the bears at once during the night when one of the bears has a bad dream and he has to come to my bedside to report, but it is difficult to haul them around the grocery store.

So he takes different ones along on our outings. He carried the littlest ones zipped inside his coat to preschool. The rest of the bears could stay home, he said, because they already know everything.

I was concerned about the little bears because Matt had said the day before that they had to go to the hospital. One of them went over a big bump when he was sledding and broke an ear and a finger, and the other bear was running and tripped on the rug and broke his nose when he hit the table. But Matt said, "It's OK to go school with broken things if they wear lots of Band-Aids."

Caring for the bears is a job Matt takes seriously. I came into the family room to find Matt and his brother Pete busily mopping up spilled water with bath towels.

"What happened?" I asked.

"The bears needed a bath, so Chewy (Matt) ran water into a plastic bag and then poured the water into this pan," Pete said.

They wanted to use the hair dryer to dry the bears' fur because the boys also had given the bears haircuts. I suggested the clothes dryer.

Matt lines all the bears up on the sofa to give them karate lessons.

MARCH

The bears always listen attentively to his instructions but they aren't very good fighters.

After all, they are teddy bears.

March 5, 1991

* * * *

Father Mac's Simple Present Warms a Heart

Mike had a fever. I know, because I took his temperature with my new thermometer.

A few weeks ago, I wrote that I never have a thermometer around. Father Aloysius McMahon, my pastor at St. Joan of Arc Catholic Church, read that column and did something about it.

A few days after the column appeared, I saw Father Mac at the Home and School book fair.

"Kathy," he said to me (Father Mac sometimes gets names confused), "can you stop over at the rectory? I got you a thermometer."

"You did?" I asked, with delight.

"I read your column, and when I saw that you don't have a thermometer because the kids break them playing hospital, I decided to get you one," he said.

"That's great, but I can't stop tonight. I have to pick up Colleen in a few minutes."

The next Sunday after Mass, Father Mac stopped John as he was walking out of church.

"John, stop over at the rectory. I've got that thermometer for you to take home."

John, who had been out of town, had not yet read the column. He had no idea what Father Mac was talking about.

Our son, Patrick, had been following John out of church. Father Mac said to him, "Mike (he gets Patrick's name confused, too, but he always comes up with a name of someone in our family), come over to the rectory to get the thermometer for your mom."

They didn't have time to stop, but they were curious.

Later, John asked me, "Did you write something about a thermometer?"

When I told him about my strep throat column, he said, "That

explains what Father Mac said."

A few days later, I was at church for a weekday Mass. It was crowded with schoolchildren and I was seated in a side pew in the back.

At the end of Mass, Father Mac spotted me. He had come in to help distribute communion and was departing up the side aisle.

"Just the person I want to see," he said, as he reached under his vestments to his shirt pocket. "This is for you."

He handed me an envelope. I opened it and found the thermometer, a note and some Lenten pamphlets.

Another day after a school Mass, Father Joe Hanefeldt, Father Mac's assistant, stopped me.

"Did Father Mac give you the thermometer?" he asked.

When I told him the tale, he said: "When Father Mac brought the thermometer home from the store, I asked him if he was sick and he said, 'No, didn't you see Kate's column? She needs a thermometer so I got one for her.' "

I've been telling this story because it's funny and because it demonstrates the importance of taking the trouble to do something for someone.

You could say that giving me a thermometer was a small gesture. But in life, it is the small gestures of kindness, of thoughtfulness, of reaching out, that make the world hum.

Father Mac is a master of the small but thoughtful gesture.

He thanks the altar boys for serving Mass. He stands at the top of the stairs and gives the sixth-graders breath mints as they pass by.

"Not because you have bad breath," he tells them, "but because I have to share."

At Mass, he remembers all the sick and suffering in the parish, and tells us to pray for them, too.

He comes to a meeting of room mothers and shakes every hand, thanking each for doing a good job. He will do this even if he already is late for his next appointment.

I tell my children, "Look beyond yourself to the world around you."

I'm happy that when they do, they find Father Mac as an example of goodness.

March 6, 1989

* * * *

Family's Place to Stow Junk
Is Kitchen Counter

The government says the dumping grounds of America are a big concern.

I hear you, Environmental Protection Agency.

I know where you're coming from, Keep America Beautiful.

That's not news to me, Department of Interior.

I've got similar problems right here in my house. Our dumping site is the end of the kitchen counter.

Everything that comes into this house spends time there first. It is our Ellis Island.

All of our stuff has to be processed across this counter before it can begin or resume a life of its own in various other locales around the house.

I'm not going to blame the accumulation on sloppy children or an absentminded husband because ours is an equal opportunity counter. It attracts my junk as well as everyone else's.

The idea to write about the conglomeration occurred to me yesterday when the counter was particularly laden with stuff.

"I should make a list of what's here for a column," I said to myself. But I didn't have time right then. Later I cleaned the counter.

When I finished I thought, "I won't be able to write about it now that all the evidence is gone."

But that was a short-lived thought. Less than a day later a new collection of stuff has appeared on our Checkpoint Charlie. To give you an idea of how this happens, I'll list a few of the items and reasons they ended up on the end of the counter.

My purse was put there when I returned from carpooling. I couldn't put it away because I don't know where it goes if it doesn't belong on the counter.

Colleen's purse also is here. I found it on the floor of the car and brought it into the house.

There is a half-written letter I want Machaela to finish so it can be mailed.

The church directory is sitting out. I used it to look up baby sitters' telephone numbers to give to another mother.

There is a dental insurance form denying a claim for Pete's checkup. The form states that his coverage ended October 21, 1984, which is his date of birth. I thought that might be because at birth he didn't need dental coverage because he didn't have any teeth. I called the insurance company. Pete was listed as my spouse and since I already have one spouse insured the insurance company dropped Pete's name from the computer.

Mike's waffle from breakfast is here. He didn't have time to finish it this morning so it was saved to eat after school. I doubt that he will eat it, but he might so it is on the counter.

There are a couple of tablets of writing paper; instructions for the strep throat medicine; a sequined headband used to play dress up; an Up With Families button I received at one of my speeches; a pair of fish earrings; and a turtle barrette in the pile

When I need to clean up in a hurry I take a grocery bag and dump everything into it except leftover waffles.

This works fine. I can sort the contents later, but for now they are out of sight.

The only danger is that sometimes the bag is mistaken for garbage; orange peels, eggshells and aluminum cans get mixed up with the yo-yo, birthday candles, bank statements, school papers, playing cards, sunglasses and a school uniform sweater.

So far, none of these bags has been accidentally carried out to the trash, and that probably never will happen because no one ever takes out the trash unless I pick up the bag, place it in his or her arms and point toward the door.

So I feel secure that I would notice my electric bill nestled among the empty cereal boxes, Indiana Jones videotape coupon and smashed milk cartons.

Even though junking our bag of junk is a temptation, we can't do it because it's junk we need. That's why it's on the kitchen counter.

March 6, 1990

* * * *

Basketball Hoop Gives Family Lots of Activity

The basketball hoop is up. It is something we have wanted to do for quite a while. Friends, who have noticed the new hoop, express surprise that we never had one before. I wanted to put one up, but I always thought first I'd have a special area paved just for basketball playing.

Well, that was one of those things on a very long list of things that I've never accomplished, and finally I started wondering why I thought that it was necessary.

I wondered,"Wouldn't a basketball hoop on the driveways edge make the house look as picture book perfect as it does when a white picket fence (which we don't have) trims the front yard."

Of course, it does, and since I'm aiming for a storybook life I decided to do it.

Everyone agreed unanimously with the idea for a hoop on the driveway. Originally, I planned to get the hoop last fall for Johnny's birthday, but the early winter blizzard discouraged the idea.

So I opted for Mike's winter birthday because the weather was unusually mild and the basketball season had begun. It also seemed to be an enticement to get the kids off the couch and away from the after-school TV shows.

I've never noticed before that there are so many basketball hoops in our neighborhood. Now that we have our own, I wonder whether we really needed it. The kids could have shot baskets at the neighbors' hoops or up at the park, but I guess it's not the same as having your own hoop.

And I enjoy shooting baskets. I'm not very good at it, even though I used to spend a lot of time as a kid at the neighbors' playing "Horse." (We didn't have a hoop. My dad said we didn't need one since the neighbors had one.) It's a game where you get a letter (H, O and so on) each time you miss when you shoot a basket.

You rotate shooting positions around the basket before making your next shot. The object of the game is to not spell horse before your opponents do. I was usually eliminated first. But our new hoop has done a lot for my basketball self-esteem. It is adjustable from heights of 7 feet to 10 feet.

I can get the ball easily through the hoop at 7 feet. So can 5-year-old Matt.

Before I went out to buy the hoop, I asked around to see what type of hoop to get. Several friends suggested buying this adjustable type. The boys' friend, Mark John, even gave me a demonstration on his hoop on how to raise and lower the hoop using the end of broom. Of course, the adjustable track on our hoop doesn't work right; it is now stuck at the 8-foot height.

John and the boys made the hoop project a weekend event. They dug the hole and mixed a bag of cement, poured it into the hole and

MARCH

then set the pole into it. They didn't know they would need a carpenter's level to make sure the pole is straight. We don't have a level, but the "men" were able to borrow one from our neighbor who came over to check out their project.

After this part was completed, the boys put their initials in the wet concrete. The girls didn't get involved, even though they like to play basketball.

"Cement writing is a male thing," Machaela said. Actually, she just didn't want to get off the phone.

They had to wait 48 hours for the concrete to set. John put together the rest of the hoop and let the backboard rest against an arm chair in the family room with the hoop and net seated on the cushion.

It remained there until the concrete was ready. When Patrick came home for spring break, he did his part and finished the job. We've been shooting hoops ever since.

March 10, 1992

* * * *

Mother Know It's Hair Today, Gone Tomorrow

Sarah Amdor's hair doesn't hang in her eyes anymore. In fact, Sarah's hair doesn't hang anywhere anymore. It stands out three-fourths of an inch around her head.

Before we go further, I should say that Sarah, my 4-year-old niece and the daughter of Mike and Cathie Amdor, still is as cute as any girl possibly could be who has sheered off her blond hair.

While the baby-sitter's back was turned, Sarah and her 5-year-old sister, Diane, went into the bathroom and used a child's scissors to perform hair surgery.

This caper took place when the girls' mother was at Sarah's preschool conference hearing how nicely Sarah's fine motor skills are developing.

"Sarah is particularly adept with the scissors," the teacher reported. When Cathie arrived home, she discovered how accurate the teacher's assessment was.

After the initial shock of seeing Sarah's hair (or lack of it), Cathie said she laughed hysterically. Now the Amdors think the new hairdo is cute. Sarah always wears or at least carries a headband or hair bow so she is not mistaken for a boy.

What is surprising is that Cathie has discovered that nearly everyone who sees Sarah has a similar story to share. I do, too.

When my teen-agers, Patrick and Colleen, were ages 3 and 2, respectively, I was in the kitchen as they busily cut up a box of tissues with scissors.

"You are making a mess," I said. "Put down the scissors and go into the other room and read a book." Even then I deluded myself, but they did leave and I continued washing dishes.

A while later I heard clipping sounds and thought, "Now they must be cutting up a plant."

I went to investigate and discovered that my plant was fine but my daughter was not. She was kneeling on the floor as agreeable as could be as Patrick enthusiastically clipped away her gorgeous hair.

She was a mess. Her bangs were gone, she had bald spots on both sides of her head, and down her back hung one section of hair - spared clipping by my intervention.

I didn't know what to do so I sat down on the couch and cried.

"She looked so pretty before," I said to Patrick, who seemed quite proud of his job, between sobs.

"I think she looks good like that," Patrick replied.

I picked up Colleen and ran next door to share the bad news. My neighbor, Janice, saw me coming and hurried out the door.

When I blurted, "Look at her," Janice laughed with relief.

"When I saw your face I thought something awful happened."

"Something awful did happen," I said. But I did reluctantly agree with Janice that it was not the end of the world.

Next I telephoned the "cut-ups' " father at his office. After I hysterically relayed the incident, he tried to calm me down by saying that it could not be as horrible as it seemed then.

When I assured him it was even worse than my description, he said, "Well, what do you want me to do? Come home and put her hair back on?"

"Do you think you could?" I asked desperately.

Colleen's hair did grow back, although not as fast as everyone said it would.

March 13, 1989

* * * *

MARCH

The Thought of Fasting
Makes Her Hungry

At the beginning of Lent, I thought I might try to fast. It seemed like it would be a good opportunity to take off the Christmas weight.

I know that's not the reason for Lenten abstinence, but I figured a little figure improvement would be a nice benefit of my penance.

Now that it is Holy Week and Easter is upon us, my motivation for Lenten sacrifice doesn't matter because my fasting ended very fast.

I barely made it through Ash Wednesday, the first day of Lent.

The no-meat-on-Friday decree which Catholics should follow during Lent hasn't been a problem. I almost always eat fish on Fridays. It has been a tradition since my childhood.

But not eating between meals is a problem. I'm glad fasting no longer is a requirement of the Catholic Church. I wonder how my parents ever kept the Lenten rules . . .

The church discontinued the fasting rule the year I turned 21, which was lucky for me because fasting was to be practiced by those 21 and older.

The fasting rule: only have meat once a day at your main meal; your two other meals combined should equal the size of your main meal. And there was to be no eating between meals.

Jeepers, just writing about fasting makes me hungry.

I suppose by today's dietary guidelines, a fast that encourages eating fish (excluding the tuna-noodle casserole which appeared regularly on Fridays on Catholic dinner tables) and not eating a lot of junk food is a good idea.

Of course, there were ways of getting around the restrictions while keeping a clear conscience.

I called Dad to see how he and Mom managed. They always seemed so good about fasting.

He said they tried but, occasionally, he would make his two small meals large, which meant his main meal had to be huge.

He said if he ate potatoes for breakfast and more potatoes for lunch, he would have had to eat 5 pounds of potatoes at his evening meal. He's Irish, and he likes potatoes.

Dad said he wasn't the only one who rationalized during Lent. A monsignor from the neighboring town was known to go to a local drugstore ice-cream fountain and order a milkshake. He said since the milkshake was a liquid, it didn't qualify as solid food.

On Saturday nights during Lent, my parents frequently entertained their friends, the Johnsons. They visited, sipped coffee and sometimes played bridge until midnight. Then Dad fixed corned beef sandwiches and served them with beer.

It was OK because it was Sunday. And on Sundays, the Lenten rules were suspended.

Mom reminded me that they only started that tradition after the rule for fasting and receiving communion had been changed.

It used to be if you planned to receive communion at a morning Mass, you had to fast from midnight on.

Lent is a time for penance, reflection and prayer in preparation for the resurrection of Jesus on Easter.

I like to make Lent a time for doing good works that might involve more effort or sacrifice than normally expended. You know, the type of things that can't be done on an empty stomach.

In case you're wondering: I never eat jelly beans until Easter morning. They taste so much better after they've been nestled in Easter basket grass.

March 26, 1991

* * * *

Styles of '70s Leave Cool Teen-Agers Cold

The favor at Maureen's Girl Scout "Beach Party Date With Someone Special" was a note in a bottle decorated to look as if it had been washed ashore. Maureen's date was her father.

This is what the note said:

Hello, Dad,

Thanks a ton for coming. I am sure it was a blast for you. No matter what you do, I will always love you. But if you start to dress like a '70s person, I will have to think about it (just kidding). But do not do it.

Love ya,

Maureen.

I think this message was inspired by our recent cleaning of the storage room.

We uncovered forgotten memorabilia - especially pictures - that we brought upstairs for John and I to reminisce over and for the kids to laugh at.

They had a great time making fun of our clothes and our hairstyles.

"Did you think those clothes were cool? You look like such nerds," was the consensus of our children.

"Mom, your hair is awful. You were a zipper head and it's feathered on the sides," they said of my Farrah Fawcett hairdo.

I looked at the same pictures and thought I looked pretty good, and most of all I looked younger, 10 or 15 years younger.

As John kept bringing more of the old things upstairs and putting them around the house, Patrick asked me, "Is Dad going to turn this into a '70s house?"

"What would be wrong with that?" I asked him.

"It reminds me of the television show, 'Welcome Back, Kotter,' when everyone dressed weird, talked weird and all the guys had weird haircuts."

The '70s are really out of style. If you say something is from the '70s, it is bad news. Fashion and interior decorating are particularly offensive.

Anything that is avocado green or harvest gold supposedly violates the eyes, but I still like those colors. They were "my colors," the ones I chose when I became engaged to be married.

I explained to my daughters that brides pick out colors so that friends can buy gifts that will match the couple's other possessions.

"You wanted presents in those colors?" Machaela asked.

"Yes, I did," I answered.

"You mean those green plates in the basement cabinets with the three small sections and the one big section? You got those as a present and you were happy about it?" Maureen wondered.

"The plates matched my fondue pot," I told them.

"They did? What's a fondue pot?" both girls asked.

I explained to my with-it daughters about the fondue fad for entertaining in the early '70s and how nice my table looked with my avocado green tablecloth, napkins and fondue pot and my gold and avocado green dishes.

"You used that yukky stuff when you had company?" Machaela said with disgust.

The generation following my generation has the same impression of the '70s as we children of the '60s had of the '50s. We thought short haircuts, big shirts and white socks were the marks of someone out of the mainstream of cool.

Now anything from the '50s and '60s is really in. The kids copy the clothes and the haircuts and love the music and dances. A '50s car - like a '57 Chevy convertible - is an ultimate cool-dude symbol.

My kids disagree, but I predict that a '70s style guy with side-burns, a wild wide tie and plaid pants, someone who listens to Donny and Marie Osmond while riding in his Pinto hatchback will be a trend-setter at parties around the year 2000.

Bell-bottom trousers will be back!

March 20, 1989

* * * *

Trouble With the Suburban
Makes Trip an Adventure

Our trip to Grand Island was an adventure, but not for the reasons we expected.

We were traveling to Grand Island for an overnight outing to see the Sandhill Cranes and for a book-signing for "Pete Goes to Grand Island." It is a story about Pete going to see the Sandhill Cranes, which stop along the Platte River to rest up and feed before migrating north.

In our entourage were 16 people: K.C. Kiner, the illustrator for all of our "Pete" books, two of her five children, seven of my eight children, my college helper, two of the kids' friends, my niece, my mother-in-law and me.

I was driving my Suburban, and K.C. was driving her minivan. Both vehicles were packed with food, coolers, warm clothes for bird-watching, boxes of books for the book signing and boxes of blue hooded sweatshirts silk-screened with Pete flying to Grand Island on the back of a Sandhill Crane.

At first, I thought the suspicious noise was coming from the kids in the back seats, but I soon realized it was coming from the engine. I hoped it would stop, but when the "service engine soon" light went on I knew I was in trouble. We chugged off to the side of the Interstate. Steam was coming out from the hood, and some green stuff was pouring out from the underside of the Suburban onto the shoulder of the road.

K.C. went for help and returned with a tow truck and two mechanics who told us the problem was much more serious than the broken hose we were hoping it would be. They mumbled something about thrown rods and spun pistons. (By the way, I had just had the Suburban serviced before setting off.)

In the middle of this gloomy scene, K.C.'s husband, Warren, with their two older daughters, drove by. They live in eastern Iowa now, and he had decided at the last minute to surprise K.C., who had come to Omaha earlier in the week, and join us in Grand Island.

I felt the angels were watching out for us when he appeared. We arranged to have the Suburban towed to Omaha. Then we transferred only the absolutely necessary stuff from the Suburban into the minivan. Warren, who was driving a small sports car, found some twine and tied some of the suitcases onto his trunk.

"Everyone put on your coat," someone suggested. "They take up too much space."

Now there were 19 of us, but we managed to all get into the minivan and the sports car for the drive to the car-rental place in Lincoln where we leased two cars for the rest of the trip. As far as I was concerned, there was no turning back and we weren't leaving anyone behind.

I didn't feel we were making the safest journey with everyone jammed into the minivan and sports car, although we drove very cautiously. But I felt a lot safer than I did when we were stranded alongside the Interstate with huge trucks barreling past us.

Eventually, we made it to Grand Island and joined the rest of our group, who already had arrived, in time to see the sunset on the Platte River, when all the Sandhill Cranes come back to the river to roost for the night. And in the morning we saw the cranes lift off from the river at sunrise. And just like Pete said in the book, it was awesome!

Plus the book-signing was a success. So all's well that ends well, which it did if I don't add up the extra expense.

March 31, 1992

* * * *

APRIL

April anticipates the arrival of Easter.
The aroma of azaleas abounds in the
abandoned flower beds. Amnesia airs
the memory of winter away. After
arm wrestling with the I.R.S. on the
fifteenth appreciate the antipasto of
life all around.

APRIL

Sunday	Monday	Tuesday	Wednesday	Thursday	Friday	Saturday
					1 Good Friday	2
3 Easter	4	5	6	7	8	9
10	11	12	13	14	15	16
17	18	19	20	21	22	23
24	25	26	27	28	29	30

APRIL

Award-Winning Book
Is an Adventure for Readers

"Who is your favorite author?" and "What is your favorite book?"

Ordinarily, I answer that I have several favorites, but I especially like reading Willa Cather's books, particularly the ones about Nebraska.

But on this day, I told the students at my book-publishing presentation that at our house we had just finished reading "Shiloh," by Phyllis Reynolds Naylor.

All the children perked up. Their teacher was reading the same book to them. "How does it turn out?" someone asked.

"Shiloh" is the recipient of the John Newbery Medal, which, according to the shiny gold seal affixed to the book, is awarded "for the Most Distinguished Contribution to American Literature for Children."

We try to read a couple chapters from a novel aloud to our four youngest children each night. Our reading time comes after the homework is completed, the book bags are organized for school, and the children are ready for bed.

Some nights the reading time gets pushed later and later because the guys are acting up. On these nights I threaten not to read because it is getting too late, but I always give in and read at least a few minutes. Mostly because I want to see what happens next in the story.

Especially in "Shiloh." None of us wanted to put the book down. One evening I was tempted to read on silently after the boys had gone to bed.

"Shiloh" is a story about a boy and a dog, not his dog but the dog he wishes was his. It also is about doing the right thing, human nature, courage and telling the truth.

But mostly it's about an 11-year old boy, Marty Preston, and Shiloh, the mistreated beagle. It is a love story. My boys would laugh if they heard me say that because they think of love stories as having lots of kissing.

Marty came from a very loving family, which made it natural for him to love Shiloh. Judd Travers, the mean owner of Shiloh, remembers his youth as a time of violence and abuse. He didn't know how to love and be kind.

We all started loving Shiloh, too. One of my favorite parts was when Marty tells about bringing Shiloh into the house for the first time:

"Bring him down the hill to the house, feed him the heels off a loaf of new bread, all the leftover sausage from breakfast, and a bowl of

milk. Then I let him lick the oatmeal pan.

"Show him every one of our four rooms, hold him in my lap on the porch swing, and laugh when he tries to stand up on the seat himself while the swing's moving. I let him smell the couch where I sleep and crawl under the front steps to sniff out the mole who lives under there, follow him all over creation when he takes out after a rabbit."

Each time we'd read, the boys would make sure our dog, Maggie, would come in and listen too. They would have Maggie climb up on the bed with us and pet her the whole time we were reading. It was like they were thinking if they were gentle with Maggie, it would make Judd Travers be nice to Shiloh in the book.

I was able to interview the author, Phyllis Reynolds Naylor, by telephone. I told her how much my family had enjoyed reading "Shiloh." She sounded as kind and gentle as I expected her to be.

Mrs. Naylor said she has written more than 70 books, including some adult novels, some picture books and numerous children's chapter books such as "Shiloh."

In reply to my question as to how she started writing books, she said, "My parents read to me as a child all the time. I always have loved books."

I don't know whether any of my children will be writing award-winning books as a result of their parents reading to them, but I know after reading "Shiloh" that they can have many wonderful adventures reading books.

April 7, 1992

* * * *

Long and Short of It: Census Takes a Little Time

That was the longest 43 minutes I have ever spent. If I had the Census Bureau's ability to stretch time, I would have a lucrative income to report on line 32-A.

Can you tell I have just filled out my census form?

The Census Bureau estimates that for the average household, this form (appropriately called the long form) should take 43 minutes to complete.

Our household is not average-sized. Even if the time allotment were doubled, I wouldn't have had enough time to complete the form.

I bet I spent 86 minutes on Question 29-B, trying to figure out my most important duties.

If you haven't seen a long-form holder lately it is not surprising. I'm sure he is busy calculating how long it took him to get to work last week and deciding if swearing in French qualifies as speaking a second language in the home. (I suppose the answer to that depends on how much swearing you do).

Even the short form is long. My neighbor thought she had the long form because she had to count the number of rooms in her house and estimate her house's resale value.

Apparently, the Census Bureau doesn't care if my neighbor has a stove and a flush toilet. The Bureau wants to know that stuff about my household, plus a lot of other things I would rather not think about.

I started the project with a positive attitude. The day I received the form, I decided I would complete it right away. I sat down at the table and scanned the form. I had heard on the news that one out of six households would receive a long form. I wasn't surprised when I realized we were among the lucky ones.

I asked myself: "What happens to you if you toss this out or bury it in a heap of papers on the kitchen counter?"

I found my answer in the instruction booklet: A census-taker will be sent to collect the information.

I didn't want that to happen, so I began filling out the form.

Question 1-A asked for the names of the people in our household - all 10 of us. I began writing. I turned the page and discovered that there was space for only seven individuals. I didn't know what to do about persons Nos. 8, 9 and 10. I forged ahead successfully until I got to the questions about yearly expenses for electricity, gas, water, oil, wood and kerosene.

I skipped those questions because they required some research.

The next segment concerned real estate taxes and homeowner's insurance. I don't like to think about these expenses when I pay them. Looking them up certainly would be no fun either.

I was about to give up the census for the evening when Patrick came around and asked: "What are you doing?"

When I explained the census, my son asked to look at the form.

"There's a whole section for you to fill out," I told him. Anyone born before April 1, 1975, has to answer the same questions as adults.

Patrick thought filling out the form would be more fun than doing his homework so he did his part.

The next day, I persuaded Colleen to complete her section. Then I

APRIL

suggested that she enter the information for the rest of the family.

She refused. "They're your kids. It's about time you counted them."

I didn't finish the form by April 1. I didn't finish adding my electricity bills until April 6.

It didn't seem like we were given much time to complete the form. The Census Bureau probably figured some folks would get the form in on time no matter what and others would get the form in late no matter what.

My philosophy: It's better late than never. I'm still doing my patriotic duty.

I thought I was keeping a census-taker away from my doorstep, but I was wrong.

I completed the final question, closed the booklet and, before I could sigh in relief, noticed a footnote.

A census-taker apparently will call me to get the information about the individuals on lines 8, 9 and 10 in Question 1-A.

Some people have all the luck.

April 10, 1990

* * * *

Actions, Not Intentions,
Finally Get Tax Forms Done

This year was going to be different. I wasn't going to be overwhelmed searching for receipts, 1099s and bank statements, all things essential to fill out the 1040A and 1040 tax forms.

This year I was going to be organized. I wasn't going to let the first two weeks of April rush past me faster than you can say "Schedule 1" as I played beat-the-clock with Wednesday's deadline for income tax filing.

But my good intentions didn't organize my charitable contributions; they didn't wade through my receipts searching for my car tax statements; and as well-intended as they might have been, these good intentions didn't add up my medical bills and subtract the insurance payments.

As is their custom, good intentions don't amount to a deduction on any line between 6a through 24c. Actions usually garner a better return just like a 401k. So I took action.

After the beginning of 1992 I began collecting all the mail which

APRIL

indicated it had something to do with the Internal Revenue Service.

I used a box that was left over from transporting my groceries from a warehouse store to house the mail stamped "important - save for income taxes."

The box was wide and long and I could easily fling into it all the W-2s, 1099s and deductible interest statements our family racked up in 1991. It sat on the floor of my office accumulating papers.

Every time I sat down to do some work I felt a kinship to the princess who had the problem sleeping on the pea. The job of reconciling last year's spending hung undone in the air surrounding me, and I couldn't relax. Although, I wonder if the source of her anxiety was not the pea but that she was anxious to marry the prince because most royalty doesn't have to file tax returns.

Finally, it was time to face the music - although I'm not sure what melody the IRS plays. I imagine a dirge would be appropriate. I went through all the checks we wrote in 1991. I put them in a pile. Then I decided to be fancy and I entered into the computer each check according to category, payee and amount. It seemed an efficient system, but it was taking too long.

I eliminated all the car repair bills when my accountant told me they weren't deductible. I argued that they should be especially when the most expensive damage occurred while I was driving to do volunteer work. I didn't want to be late so I ignored the telltale warning lights, which I now know indicate imminent catastrophe. Apparently, stupidity isn't deductible either. Too bad.

How about expenses incurred while undergoing temporary insanity? I had a lot of those. For example, what about the night we made two orders of takeout Chinese food. Shouldn't one of these dinners for 10 be deductible? I think we were working on 1990's taxes that night and not intellectually engaged.

What about the disastrous clothing purchases? Shouldn't the outfits I bought for my girls for Christmas that were worn just long enough to make me happy and worn too long to be returned be deductible?

OK, how about a deduction for the new clothes I bought for myself? A girl's got to have something nice to wear in case she's called in for an audit. Right?

April 14, 1992

* * * *

Mice in the House
Are Driving Mistress Batty

If you have a squeamish stomach it might be good to stop reading right now. If I didn't need to go through a catharsis by talking about it, I wouldn't.

We have caught 16 mice. Cinderella's only friends were mice and in children's stories, mice often are the heroes. I like those books, but I am terrified of mice in my house.

This house de-mousing has been going on for more than two weeks. They hang out in the drawer beneath my cook top.

We realized we had mice when our cat's natural instinct prevailed and he presented us with the evidence. I thought, "Good, the cat got the mouse."

The next day my heartbeat escalated when I was emptying the dishwasher and discovered a mouse that had not survived the pot-and-pan cycle. I almost didn't survive that incident; I mistook the mouse's well-washed insides for mashed bananas and cleaned them out with my fingers.

Colleen bought traps, but I was afraid I'd snap my fingers off while I was spreading on the peanut butter. Colleen's friend, Sara, offered to set them for me.

I went to bed that night believing I lived in a mouseless house or that the mouse was houseless. It was a short-lived feeling. In the morning, the trap we had set was empty. It had no mouse and no bait.

I can't empty or dispose of the traps once they've done their jobs. I can't even check the drawer to see if the traps have worked. The job has been delegated to anyone I can persuade to do it.

Ten-year-old John is the designated de-mouser. After a few days of this icky job, he said he is not sure he wants to be "the man of the house." Maureen's friend, Bridget, who helped baby sit one night, has emptied a trap.

Amy, my college-aged helper, came in one morning, looked in the drawer and confirmed the mouse's presence. But she said unloading traps wasn't in her job description.

The plumber did and reset the trap for another catch.

When Machaela and I were returning from an errand Amy yelled from my bedroom window, "Kate, watch out. The cat is chasing a mouse around the family room."

I hurried in with the idea of dodging the cat-and-mouse game and

running right upstairs. En route I had to confront the two of them as the mouse scampered into the dining room, where I was planning to entertain that evening.

Our weekend house guest, Bill, got involved. He set the traps to catch three mice in the two days he was here. Our count was up to eight. I was convinced that had to be the last of them.

My life has been consumed with these mice. A paper fluttered off the counter onto the floor and I flinched because I thought it was a mouse passing by. I got the dictionary to look up a word and opened the book to "capybara," a 4-foot-long rodent. There even was a picture of it. It looked like a huge mouse.

I couldn't sleep without dreaming of a mouse invasion or, worse yet, a capybara invasion.

Finally, I thought I had been liberated of them. But once again my celebration ended as quickly as a good mousetrap springs into action.

We couldn't catch anything in the traps. I summoned all my courage and cleverness to bait the traps. I put the peanut butter on heavily, on lightly, only on top of the trigger and then only on the bottom.

I called an exterminator. He suggested wadding up a cotton ball with peanut butter in it. I did and hooked it onto the trap so securely I thought the mouse never would get it off, but it did every time.

The exterminator also suggested a different brand of trap. I bought five. They worked. I bought eight more the next morning.

I have six left. There are two set in the drawer and four in a bag on the counter. If we use all of these traps I'll surrender and consider taking mice, mouse traps and peanut butter as income tax deductions next year.

April 16, 1991

* * * *

Sweat Pants, T-Shirts Beat PJ's Any Day

Mike was getting ready for a slumber party. He was excited because he had never stayed overnight at a friend's house before. I was helping him pack his gear.

"Why don't you take these Chinese pajamas?" I asked, holding up the freshly laundered and folded pair.

"No, I don't want to."

"How about the dinosaur ones? They should still fit," I said, digging in the drawer.

"No. Do you know where those cut-off sweat pants and my Turtle T-shirt are? I'll take them to sleep in," my son responded.

"Don't you think you should take pajamas?" I asked.

"Why?"

Why, indeed, I said to myself. He never wears pajamas at home; neither do his brothers. They sleep in T-shirts and shorts in warm weather and sweat suits in the winter.

If most households are like ours, and I imagine a lot of them are, the pj industry for the size 6 and above set must be in a recession. But again, maybe it's not. There are still mothers like me who keep tradition and buy pj's even though they are never or seldom worn.

Sometimes, my guys will put on their pajamas after their evening showers. The boys look so nice and fresh and neat. But most of the time, they scrounge around looking for something well-worn and comfortable to sleep in.

I guess this is OK as long as they don't reach for the dirty clothes they just took off.

I read a parenting article in which an expert on children suggested that parents let children wear the same knit clothing to school as they wore to bed the night before.

If we did that, we would have to find something else to argue about in the morning.

My guys can't understand why I won't let them wear the clothes they've worn continuously since school let out on Friday to church on Sunday. They also don't understand why they have to take showers when they just took them three days earlier.

I usually win this argument when I point out that the tomato sauce stains on their shirts Sunday morning came from the pizza we had Friday night.

My guys like to stay up until they drop or I start having a fit because they are still awake (which ever happens first). They flop into bed after performing minimalistic hygiene rituals in the bathroom.

Their sense of style does save money, since I never feel tempted to purchase a cute ensemble displayed in a store window.

Mike and John's favorite tops for playing and sleeping are the sweat shirts I bought for them last fall from a vendor at the loading dock of the ferry for the Statue of Liberty in New York City. It was

APRIL

the end of the day, and he was slashing prices.

Pete alternates wearing his two elves sweat shirts, which were made to promote my book, "I Can't Sleep With Those Elves Watching Me."

Matt likes his purple or black sweat shirt.

They all wear sweat pants with holes in the knees. I've been gradually cutting off the sweat pants to make shorts, but not without protest. They argue that if I cut off too many sweat pants, they won't have anything to wear after school on cool days.

I guess the boys like to keep their ankles warm, even if their knees can feel the evening breezes.

When my older kids were little, I was embarrassed if they were seen dressed like that. My standards have lowered - dramatically. Now, it doesn't really matter what they wear when they're asleep or awake. I always tell them, "You are cute and that's what is important."

April 23, 1991

* * * *

'Safety Nut' Sounds Smoke-Detector Warning

It was Good Friday, late in the evening. I was sitting in the family room of my childhood home, talking with my sister, Sheila.

She was trying to coax her little one, Ned, into bed but he wasn't interested. He had more important business: ripping, tossing and stuffing newspapers which had been piled on the coffee table.

Just when we thought we were the only ones awake, we were startled by a loud, wailing noise.

"Isn't that the smoke alarm?" I asked Sheila.

"It sounds like it," she answered.

The alarm stopped as abruptly as it started. I decided to pinpoint the reason. Just then, my Dad walked into the room. He was wearing his pajamas and carrying a pole.

"Did I scare you?" he asked, smiling sheepishly.

"Was that the smoke detector?" I asked.

"Yes, I was testing it to make sure the batteries were good." (That was the purpose of the pole. He used it to reach the testing button.)

He had intended to test the alarms before his family had arrived for the Easter weekend.

APRIL

"I was just about to get in bed when I remembered and decided I had better do it now. Otherwise, I'd wake up at 2 a.m. and wouldn't be able to get back to sleep until I tested the batteries."

My father and I think alike. Last summer, before my husband and I took our older kids to Europe, I tested the smoke alarms at our house.

We installed new batteries and tested each smoke detector to make sure the batteries weren't duds.

Two detectors lack testing buttons, so we had to improvise by lighting a candle and blowing it out so that the smoke would waft toward the sensor.

When the alarm sounded, I hastily fanned the smoke with a folded newspaper.

We took these steps because I didn't want to become panicked on our trip if it occurred to me that more than half of my children were thousands of miles away, asleep in a house equipped with non-functional smoke detectors.

My main floor detector used to go off every time I used the broiler. Each time, I considered it a good signal for me to blow off steam.

I recently retested all the smoke detectors in our home, with Maureen's help. She thought it was fun. I thought it was noisy.

When I was young - before smoke detectors were invented - my dad conducted fire drills. My older sister and I were supposed to get the little girls and climb out a window onto the porch roof.

Smoke detectors are my thing. A while ago, Grandma Cavanaugh invited the grandchildren to her house for a slumber party. (Grandma loves to entertain the kids by making leprechauns dance on the walls and cooking pancakes.)

As I drove the children to Grandma's house, I thought, "This is quite a crowd for Grandma but they should get along fine if everyone is in good spirits and the big kids help with the little kids."

I decided to stop en route and buy a new battery for the smoke alarm in Grandma's house. I installed the battery and tested the alarm with a lighted candle.

My mother-in-law thanked me. The kids called me a "safety nut."

The next day, I read a heartbreaking newspaper story about a fire which could have been avoided if the house had had a smoke detector in working order.

Ordinarily, I don't use this space as a soap box. But smoke detectors save lives. I think every residence - including college dorm rooms and apartments - should be equipped with working smoke detectors.

If you have a smoke detector, test the battery. If the battery is dead, replace it immediately.

If you don't have a smoke detector, buy one. They are inexpensive. I'll sleep a lot better if I know you are safe.

April 24, 1990

* * * *

Baby's Birth Adds to Count Of Blessings

When the telephone rang, I was arranging flowers, my mother was wrapping silverware and my dad was marinating the meat for the evening's festivities.

I left what I was doing and went to pick up the receiver. At first I didn't recognize the voice, but when I did, I was excited.

"Did you have the baby?" I hurriedly asked my sister, Sheila. When she answered that she did, I screeched and my mother came running and Dad stopped what he was doing at the stove.

"Sheila had the baby," I told my parents.

"Boy or girl? And when?" I asked.

"A boy born about an hour ago?" I repeated into the phone.

"How is he? How are you? How's Ken (my sister's husband)?"

"Wonderful, wonderful, wonderful," my sister answered to all three questions. "We are calling him William Ned."

It was a time to rejoice - as it always is when a new and healthy life makes its debut into our world. But our family had even more reason to be excited, pleased and thankful with the new son, grandson, nephew and cousin.

Sheila and Ken lost a baby 14 months ago. The baby was an almost full-term stillborn girl. We were heartbroken when it happened. They named her Sheila Maureen.

My family is used to good things happening; so when the baby died it seemed like one of our expected blessings was denied.

It wasn't supposed to be like that. It was sad and hard to accept. But life continues and so did Sheila, Ken and Max, their 2-year-old son.

At the summer get-together at the lake, Ken won the Bert Johnson Invitational, the family's 8-mile run to Lake Geneva City. And at a talent show organized by the children, Sheila, Ken and Max

APRIL

77

performed in a goofy skit as the king, queen and prince of Hungie Bungie.

Then the good news came. A new baby was expected in early April.

The happy anticipation began and continued as Sheila's due date approached and passed.

Also on the agenda was the celebration party for my book, to which I had invited my parents. Sheila and my parents live in the Chicago area. Mom and Dad wanted to come but also wanted to be on hand to help with Max in case Sheila gave birth.

Another sister, Bonnie, interceded and went to stay with my sister and Ken. I had my party, Sheila had the baby the same day, and happiness filled the air.

That is the way life is supposed to be.

The joy little William Ned's birth has given our family would be no less if we had not lost his sister last year. But because we did, our joy is so much more abundant.

Both occasions have reminded us of the fragility of the gifts we continually receive. Life, love, family and friendship are the treasures of the world.

We never will forget Sheila Maureen and the missed opportunity to know her. Her memory has blessed all the Barretts with renewed joy and faith as we welcome her brother.

And on the Cavanaugh side of the family, the blessings are overflowing. We celebrated the November 5 birth of Claire Irene Boyer, the March 30 birth of Bertilla Bernadette Cavanaugh and await the impending June birth of Baby Amdor.

The flowers of spring are blooming; the garden is beautiful.

April 24, 1989

* * * *

Loads of Luck In Washer Flood

Let me set the scene - it's one of calm before the storm - meaning the downpour in my entry hall. I was upstairs getting my little guys ready for bed. I said I would read to them, but first I wanted to put the school uniforms in the washer, which is upstairs near the bedrooms. I started the machine and then went to Pete and Matt's room to read.

Then the phone rang. I went downstairs to the kitchen phone because the caller was giving me information I needed to write on the calendar. While I was talking I heard the rushing sound of water. I peered into the entry hall and saw water pouring out of the ceiling light fixture.

I ended my call and ran upstairs to the laundry room, where the water already was an inch deep and rising fast.

I quickly turned off the machine thinking that would stop the flow. It didn't. Instead, it continued to squirt out wildly from the washer hose. The water was very hot, and the laundry area was like a steam room at an athletic club.

I knew I had to get behind the dryer to shut off the faucets. First, I thought, I should unplug the dryer, but I didn't want to be electrocuted. I climbed atop the washer to pull out the dryer's cord from the outlet.

By this time, the kids had arrived at the scene to see what was going on. I was trying to shut off the water at the faucet, but the hot water was making the faucet too hot to handle. I had Maureen hold a towel on the leaking hose so I could do it, but even that didn't help. The water kept shooting out around the towel and through it.

Meanwhile, as Maureen and I were getting our clothes soaked and our hair curled from the the steam bath, Machaela, Mike and Johnny were putting pans and towels on the entry hall floor.

I decided I would have to turn off the water for the house. One time, my dad showed me where the shut off faucets were should something like this happen. Now I couldn't remember if the shutoffs were behind the furnace, under the sink or by the water meter. All I knew is that they were in the basement.

I ran from faucet to faucet trying to figure it out. Every time I tried one I yelled to Pete, who was waiting at the top of the basement stairs so he could yell to Maureen who was still holding the towel to see if I found the right one. Finally, she said the water was subsiding. I ran back upstairs and was able to get the other faucets turned off.

What a mess! Every towel, plus the load of clean laundry I had set on the floor with the intention of folding right after I read to the boys, was soaked. The school uniforms were sitting in the filled washing machine tub. After I turned the water back on I had to rinse them in the bath tub, wring them out and hang them up to dry because they needed to be worn to school the next morning.

After everything calmed down again Mike said, "that was fun."

The next day when the plumber came to fix the damaged hose, he told us how lucky we were.

"It could have been a lot worse. If you weren't home to get the water turned off you would really have had a disaster," he said.

As I looked at the water-soaked and stained entry hall-ceiling, the shorted-out light fixture and piles of soaked laundry, I thought, "Boy, I guess I'm just one of those people with all the luck."

April 27, 1993

* * * *

Trash Bag Must Suffice as Easter-Trip Luggage

Pete arranged his clothes on his bed as we prepared for our Easter trip to Illinois to see Grandpa and Grandma. He was bringing several pairs of sweat pants, some with holes in the knees, and his good pair to wear if he went somewhere.

He packed short-sleeved shirts and not any "sleeved" shirts, which is what he calls long-sleeved shirts that he won't wear because he doesn't like his arms to be confined. He told me I was in charge of packing his Easter clothes and he wondered whether he would be able to change right after church.

When Pete, who is 7, asked for a suitcase for his clothes, I told him to get a trash bag and we would pack his and Matt's clothes in it. That idea didn't go over with him.

"How come I always have to use a trash bag for my stuff?" he asked.

"You do?" I asked.

"When we went to Grand Island to see the Sandhill Cranes, I did," he told me.

His older brothers, John and Mike, found an Army duffel bag for their clothes, and Pete wanted to use something similar. I began searching around for some other kind of bag for Pete. But we seem to be in a suitcase downturn. The girls had already laid claims on what was available that didn't have broken zippers or latches.

Pete said it is embarrassing to bring his clothes in a trash bag. Colleen tried to influence him otherwise.

"No one will even see it," she told him. "When we arrive it will be dark. I'll carry it in for you, and besides, a trash-bag suitcase takes

up less space in the car because it is soft and fits in smaller spaces."

I resorted to bribery.

"If you use the trash bag this time, I'll get you a suitcase of your own to use for your next trip."

I'm not sure whether he believed me, but the weekend passed with no more discussion about his traveling bags.

Pete didn't need to wear his "sweat pants for going places." Most of our Chicago sightseeing trips were canceled because of what they were referring to in Chicago as "da flood" caused by "da hole."

In case you missed it, before Easter weekend the basements of Chicago's Loop were flooded by Chicago River water gushing into a series of tunnels under the downtown area. Electricity and water were also turned off.

Matt had hoped to make his first trip to the top of the Sears Tower. For my guys, everything in life is compared to the Sears Tower. Whenever they see a tower, a tall person, a Lego block construction, or an airplane flying overhead they wonder how it compares in height to the Sears Tower. Making that long elevator ride to the top of the Sears Tower is the Mount Everest climbing challenge of Matt's 5-year-old life, but he had to put it off until his next visit.

When it was time to pack up to drive home to Omaha, I wondered why we brought so much stuff we didn't need or use. I think we could have easily put everything our whole family needed into one trash bag - but it's a good thing we didn't because I left Pete's traveling trash bag behind.

As convenient as it is to use a trash bag as a suitcase, there is one drawback. It can easily be thought to contain what it was intended to contain: trash.

As we packed up, I had the kids set our stuff by the back door of my parents' home. Pete's trash bag was put on top of the recycling basket by the back door. I thought it was filled with empty pop cans, so we left it there, but I thought wrong. I should have recognized it not as a trash bag at all but one piece from the matched set of luggage stored in the cardboard box under my kitchen sink.

Grandpa discovered our oversight after we departed. Now I'm wondering how a trash-bag suitcase will travel by mail.

April 28, 1992

* * * *

MAY

May greets us with the generosity of spring and a glistening glow on the lilac bush. The gardens grow geraniums, the grass grows green, and gardenias grace prom gowns. Graduates glide out into life with glittering glee and mothers are given gifts of glamour and good will.

MAY

Sunday	Monday	Tuesday	Wednesday	Thursday	Friday	Saturday
1	2	3	4	5	6	7
8 Mother's Day	9	10	11	12	13	14
15	16	17	18	19	20	21
22	23	24	25	26	27	28
29	30 Memorial Day	31				

MAY

Turtles Prove Times Change, Toys Mutate

My dad tells the story about me at the age of 3 teaching a friend to make the sign of the cross by saying: In the name of the Father, the Son, and Kukla, Fran and Ollie.

Kukla, Fran and Ollie probably was the first program on television for children. It is a far cry from the sophisticated programming of the '80s, but it was exciting for me.

As a mother, I have been through the Gilligan's Island phase when Patrick turned his bedroom into Gilligan's Island and had to sleep in the hallway. And I've been through the Dukes of Hazzard era when everyone in the neighborhood had a Dukes' T-shirt and we had a replica of the General Lee, the Dukes' car.

The He-Man and Skelator period began at our house when Mike, who couldn't even talk yet, charged around the house with a mitten on his outstretched hand and He-Man's sword stuffed down the back of his shirt.

We collected all the He-Man and She-ra (He-Man's sister) characters. We still have them, but they are buried in the toy cabinet and most have suffered a lost limb, head or armored chest plate.

The Ghostbusters still are popular. My guys like the cartoon show and like to play Ghostbusters. Mike received a Ghostbusters toy for his birthday, and he also received a Teen-age Ninja Mutant Turtle. Action Figures

It seems that we now are in the Renaissance era of toys. The Teen-age Ninja Mutant Turtles are named Michaelangelo, Raphael, Donatello and Leonardo.

Suddenly my life is filled with turtles. The Teen-age Ninja Mutant Turtles' motto is: "One good turtle deserves another," which also became John, Mike, Pete and Matt's creed. They felt an urgency to have all of the turtles - the good, the bad and the accessories.

The Teen-age Mutant Ninja Turtles have a history that I discovered by reading the packaging surrounding the action figures.

According to legend, the turtles evolved when a boy's bowl of pet turtles fell into the stench of an underground city sewer. The turtles landed on Splinter, a penniless but powerful Ninja master who lived in the muck.

Splinter's enemy, Shredder (leader of the evil Foot Clan), poured disgusting green ooze over Splinter and, accidentally, the turtles, hoping to kill Splinter. Instead, the pet turtles mutated into teen

turtles and Splinter turned into the biggest rat ever to face a trap.

Splinter taught the turtles the ways of the Ninja. Together they formed a team for the side of good against the deadly Foot Clan, which is headed by Shredder. The Foot Clan's motto is, "The only good turtle is soup."

The vital statistics of Raphael, the witty voice of the turtles, are:

Birthplace: Shelly's Pet City, New Hampshell.

Height: 5 foot, 1 inch.

Weight: 147 pounds, with shell.

Age: 15 (people years).

Shell: Hard as old chewing gum.

Weapons: Turtle fist daggers.

Splinter, the leader of the turtles, wears a Ninja robe over his oversized rat body. Mike recently received a similar robe as a hand-me-down from some friends. Mike says he likes wearing the robe because Splinter wears one and because he says rich people wear robes like it.

The turtles are careful about confronting people because they say, "When it comes to turtles, humans just don't know what's going on. Present company excluded." They are referring to April O'Neil, the news reporter who gets in all the turtles' predicaments and also drives the Turtle Mobile for them.

The existence of 4 1/2-foot Teen-age Mutant Ninja Turtles, who are too young to drive and only eat pizza, made me curious so I called Mirage Studios in Northampton, Massachusetts, where the turtles are made and I talked to Cheryl Trindle, Ninja Turtle spokeswoman, to find out more about them.

The Ninja Turtles were created by artists Kevin Eastman and Peter Laird in 1984 after they spent an evening watching bad television. They drew a turtle with a bandana over his eyes, and the rest evolved.

The creators gave the turtles names of Renaissance artists because the inventors had studied the artists' works and admired them. As it turned out, Splinter also was an admirer of the Renaissance painters.

The creators developed a Teen-Age Ninja Mutant Turtle comic book, distributed it along the East Coast and achieved quick success. Eventually, the comic books developed into the action figures which we have in abundance, and a television cartoon show and videotapes that we frequently view.

In the Ninja Turtle world, it is a struggle of good versus evil. The good, of course, are the turtles and their leader, Splinter. The evil is Shredder. Shredder is a human but his foot soldiers were created by stealing a wart hog and a rhinoceros from the zoo and joining them with a foot soldier by using Shredder's mutantage formula. The result was Bebop and Rocksteady, who have brute strength and the ability to think.

The turtles and Splinter always are victorious in these confrontations. That is why they are known as "heroes in a half shell."

May 1, 1989

* * * *

Tricks Can Make Capital of Geography

The woman on the telephone was giving me the address for her company. I had called a toll-free number, so I didn't know where she was located. When she said Indianapolis, I couldn't control myself. I had to say, "That's the capital of Indiana."

She said, "Yes, it is," and continued the mailing directions. "If you have any questions about your order, call our toll-free number and ask for Rochelle."

"Is that you?" I wondered.

"No, it's my daughter," she replied.

"Oh, that's nice. Does she work with you right there in Indianapolis?"

"Yes, it is nice," she answered "She just moved here from Nashville."

"Oh, she came from Nashville, the capital of Tennessee," I repeated.

I have state capitals on my mind because Mike recently had to learn the states and capitals for geography class. Since he is my sixth child, I should know all the capitals by now, but every time one of my children has this assignment, it's a new learning experience.

There are some capitals that I can never keep straight. If I hear the name for the capital city I can usually put it with the state, but if I have to come up with the name for the capital on my own I'm stumped.

How about you? Can you name the capitals of Nevada, South Carolina, New Hampshire, Michigan and Missouri? I wouldn't be

able to if I hadn't just finished studying them.

We tried all sorts of creative ways to help Mike learn the states and capitals. I entered all the states, their capitals and their section of the country on the computer. Then I had the computer print various arrangements of the states and capitals so Mike could learn by matching them up.

My husband said Mike should be using a map while he studied. That made sense, so we found the U.S. map in his geography book. Then Machaela reminded me of all the tricks I used to help her remember. Some of them are farfetched but they must have worked because she still remembers them four years later.

Her favorite one is: "My friend, Louise, wears rouge when she throws the baton." This is the clue for Baton Rouge, the capital of Louisiana.

I taught Mike to think of the rich man from Virginia who goes to West Virginia to dance the Charleston as a way to remember Richmond, the capital of Virginia, and Charleston, the capital of West Virginia.

"Dad and Matt's birthdays are in August and Mike Kelly (their friend) lives in Maine." I don't know why this clue - that Johnny made up for Augusta, the capital of Maine - worked, but it did.

We studied the capitals in the car while driving to practices and in the kitchen, while we were fixing dinner. If I'd see Mike as he walked through the room, I would name a state and he would say the capital and then keep on walking.

Sometimes I'd get the boys mixed up and I would ask the wrong guy to name a capital. But apparently they were all learning, because a lot of times I'd get a correct answer from the wrong student.

How did Mike do on the test? Great! Now we can put that episode behind us until Pete gets into the fourth grade.

By the way, the answers to my little quiz are Carson City, Nevada; Columbia, South Carolina; Concord, New Hampshire; Lansing, Michigan; and Jefferson City, Missouri.

May 4, 1993

* * * *

 **MAY**

She Talks, She Mops
and She Glows at Results

My mother always says, "You can't get your housework done talking on the telephone."

Since I now talk, think and act like my mother, I say that too. But it isn't always true. Sometimes, I get a lot of housework done while talking on the telephone.

For example, during a recent conversation with my friend, Kathy, I washed the kitchen baseboards while she prepared a pork roast.

I probably wouldn't have cleaned the baseboards that day if Kathy had not called.

As we talked, I noticed a spot on the floor and grabbed a wet dishcloth from the sink. One spot led to another and before I knew it I was crawling on the floor, attacking the scummy corners and baseboards.

It helps to have a phone with a long cord - or a cordless phone. I had a cordless phone, but I had trouble with it so I stopped using it. For some reason, radio station KFAB came over the line.

Every time I picked up the phone, I thought I had been put on hold because I heard music.

A long cord on our kitchen phone allows me a lot of leeway. One recent morning, I cleaned the refrigerator and organized the pantry shelves while I talked on the telephone with another mother. We rehashed the antics of our teen-agers and commiserated about today's high prices for everything.

When Kathy answers her phone, she sometimes lays a wet towel on the floor and shuffles around the kitchen, mopping as she goes. She gets three things done at once: cleaning, talking and exercising.

Some things are difficult or impolite to do while you're on the telephone. I do wash dishes and talk, but I don't run the garbage disposal or vacuum.

Taking a shower, playing the trombone, eating peanut butter on crackers and engaging in romantic interludes are to be avoided during telephone conversations, too.

Yelling at your kids isn't polite when you are on the phone, but sometimes it can't be helped. Shooing your children by waving dramatically or mouthing threats that predict bodily harm are minimally effective.

Folding laundry is a good thing to do while talking on the telephone. It's a quiet task and doesn't require a lot of thinking.

I usually fold clothes in the master bedroom, where we have a desk-top telephone with a short cord. I usually watch television or listen to the radio if I don't have any calls to make.

If the phone should ring, I'm glad for the distraction. Whenever I stretch the telephone cord in an attempt to shut off the radio or television, I run into trouble.

The phone invariably falls off the nightstand and the call is disconnected, or the phone plug comes out of its socket and I have to move the bed away from the wall to reinsert the four-pronged adapter. (It always takes at least four stabs.)

If it is especially noisy in our kitchen, I stretch the telephone cord into the powder room and close the door.

When I do this, I say I am in my office. I can hear what's being said and scour the bathroom fixtures.

It's a good thing we don't have one of those phones where the caller can see me on a television screen.

May 1, 1990

* * * *

Mom Forever Asking: 'Do I Make Myself Clear?'

"Mom, can I take the car and go to the bank?" Colleen asked.

"Wait a minute, as soon as I finish getting this package ready I'm going to take it to the post office. We'll go together."

Then I had another thought, "Campbell is leaving in a few minutes, she can drop me off at the post office, you can go ahead to the bank and then pick me up." I even think I added "I'll be waiting for you in front of the post office."

What do you suppose happened as a result of this conversation? Did I make myself clearly understood? Before we analyze this dialogue, let me tell you what happened.

About 15 minutes after Colleen left in my car, Campbell dropped me off at the post office. I mailed my package and went back outside to wait for Colleen. It was about 4:50 p.m.

At first, I entertained myself by watching people drive up to the lines of mailboxes and attempt to get their bundles of letters into the

correct box (without having to get out of the car). One guy dropped his letters on the ground and had to open his car door and get out to retrieve them.

Another woman couldn't decide if she had letters for the metered mailbox, the out-of-town box or local mail. She kept shifting the gears of her car from reverse to forward as she rolled between the boxes.

A third person, driving a four-wheel drive vehicle similar to mine and equipped with large side-mirrors, had the same problem I have when I try to maneuver close enough to reach the mailbox without tearing the mirror off the door.

It was 4:58 p.m.

Mike had baseball practice at 5 o'clock. I called home on a pay phone to tell Maureen to walk him over to the park. "I'll be home in a few minutes," I told her and then I hurried back to my post to wait for my ride.

I began reading the front pages of the newspapers in the street vendor cases. I considered purchasing one and dug around the bottom of my purse for more change but I didn't have enough.

Next I engaged in a fretting game. I thought of all the things I could be doing at 5:15 p.m. if I wasn't standing in front of the post office.

"Should I start walking?" I asked myself. "But when Colleen comes she won't find me and I'll get in trouble because I didn't stay put. Well, I can watch for her as I walk." I did this on my two-mile walk home.

Luckily, I like to walk and I was dressed for it. When I got to the house no one had heard from, or seen, Colleen.

"She's going to kill me. She's probably driving all around searching for me," I thought. Just as I decided I better take the other car and go back to the post office, Colleen pulled up. I braced myself for the onslaught of "Where were you?" questions. But she just said "hi" and headed into the house.

Finally, I asked "Were you looking for me?"

"Looking for you? No, why? Where were you?" she asked.

"At the post office, you were supposed to pick me up."

"Oh, I thought Campbell was taking you. I figured if you wanted me to pick you up you would have given me more detailed instructions like you always do."

What we have here is a failure to communicate!

All the computer programs, fax machines and cellular phones technology can manufacture won't make a dent in the problems of getting your point across in a family. Messages and conversations always will be misinterpreted, not heard or not received.

I complain about my children not listening to me but they say, "You never listen to us and then get mad because you're supposed to know something that we tried to tell you a zillion times but you always said, 'tell me later.'"

Right now, it is likely that there is a whole bunch of stuff I'm supposed to know about that no one wants me to know and, as a mother of teen-agers, I think it is probably better that way.

May 8, 1990

* * * *

What's The Topic? I Forget . . .

As I was driving, I got an idea to write my next column about forgetting.

I dismissed the idea after a couple of blocks because I didn't think I had enough to develop a column, and I couldn't think of any other recent situation in which forgetting about something could be used as an anecdote.

However, it's very possible that I've forgotten something and I don't even know about it.

For example, what if I am of royal lineage in some obscure country and I won't remember until I get a decree that I'm next in line to the throne?

Or what if I forgot that I once worked as a hoochie-koochie dancer in a burlesque house? And I forgot that all the sequined costumes in the back of the closet are not from my daughters' dance recitals but from my former job?

I won't recall that job until I find a faded news clipping, recounting my arrest by the vice squad, lining the bottom of my lingerie drawer.

Far-fetched, you say? Why not? Stuff such as that happens every day on soap operas. Those people are really forgetful.

I won't rule out either of the above situations as possibilities of something I've forgotten, but since I couldn't remember if I forgot them it didn't make sense to write about them.

So I decided to write about something else - but now I've forgotten what that was.

My drive was to church to hear Pete read in the school Mass. There was little chance that I would forget to be there since he reminded me

hourly the evening before.

But during the Mass, perhaps in a bolt of divine guidance, I remembered that I was supposed to be at Matt's preschool in an hour to read from my books.

I was so relieved that I remembered then instead of later after I had forgotten. I always get this feeling of intense gratitude when I remember something that I was supposed to do before it is too late and it goes into the "I Forgot" file.

Sometimes, though, I wish I would forget things. It would be an explanation for not doing things that I don't want to do. It would be embarrassing to have to admit you forgot but it's better than feeling guilty for blowing something off.

But I never forget to do those things. I try, but there's always an annoying reminder nagging in the back of my brain that doesn't let me off the hook.

Sometimes I remember and forget something several times in the space of a couple of minutes.

Sometimes I'll answer the phone in my bedroom, listen carefully to what the caller has to say, even make comments or suggestions, and then hang up the phone and completely forget all about the conversation by the time I walk down stairs.

It's maddening when I go into a room for a reason and then forget why I'm there.

I made a half of a turkey sandwich in the kitchen and walked back into my den and continued my vacuuming while I was eating it (someone was coming over in 10 minutes and I needed to get the place cleaned up in a hurry).

I finished eating the half-sandwich and the vacuuming and decided I was still hungry so I went to the kitchen to make another half. In the meantime, the phone rang, I wiped off the counters, read a pizza advertisement and looked at pictures from my daughters' Field Day before I thought about the second half of the sandwich again.

Then I couldn't remember if I had already made and eaten the sandwich or I hadn't. I couldn't tell if I was still hungry or not.

Did I make another half-sandwich just in case I hadn't before and I was still hungry?

I'd tell you if I knew, but I forgot.

May 12, 1992

* * * *

House-Breaking Strains
Owner-Dog Relationship

I had just returned from my walk when my life changed.

The kids spotted me as I walked up the sidewalk. They all ran out of the house as if the someone had set off a stink bomb and they had to scramble for fresh air. All at once, I caught an earful of why they were so excited.

"Tommy called and he has a puppy. Can we get it?"

I walked into the house shaking my head no.

"You're supposed to call him," they told me. To be polite, I decided I would call Tommy, my oldest son's friend, to tell him I didn't want a puppy. I should have written him a letter.

"What's the story about the puppy?" I asked him.

"I got this puppy at the Humane Society and my roommates and I just moved to a different place and we can't keep her," he told me. "If you don't take her I'll have to take her back to the pound."

"Isn't there anyone else to take her?" I inquired, not believing my ears as I heard those words.

"No," he answered. "She's a great dog too."

Even though I had planned to be off the phone by now, with this incident placed in the past, I slid right into another question.

"What kind of dog is she ?" I asked, feigning the casual interest of someone one might meet out on the street. However, the stranger eventually moves on. I didn't. Instead, I felt as if some giddy sap had taken over my body's good-sense mechanism.

"She's a mix - a golden retriever and springer spaniel. She's really pretty and she has great eyes." Tom told me.

Then, I uttered the words which clinched the deal. Words Tom and I both knew were bound to send me shopping for a leash and collar the next day and into the vet's office the day after that.

"Bring her over so I can see her." I knew I was getting a dog.

Before I could reconsider, Tom and his brother, David, were on our front lawn, with the puppy they called Rookie. Tom was right: She was really pretty, very good-natured, affectionate and not too rambunctious. The color of her coat matched our cat's fur and blended nicely with all the redheads in our family. I fell in love.

That was a month ago and I admit the love affair is still going, but my puppy has tested our relationship on almost every level.

We changed her name to Maggie Rose. It was the name I chose. I

thought she should have a girl's name.

Since Maggie has come into our lives, I've wondered what I talked about before I had a dog. I never felt at a loss for words before, but now the only conversations I can participate in are about my dog. I'm consumed with my puppy's personal habits. I'm in awe of anyone who has house-trained a dog successfully and I seek out those people for advice. The piece of advice I earnestly hope is true came from my dad.

"She'll get trained in spite of you," he told me.

I feel like I have a toddler in the house again. In addition to the problem mentioned above, Maggie gets into everything and chews whatever is handy. I constantly am pulling something out of her mouth - sometimes the clothes I am wearing. She bites the broom and barks at the vacuum cleaner. But she is so lovable and I know she does want to please us. I hope she figures out how soon.

I got eight children successfully through this stage, I should be able to get one puppy trained.

Shouldn't I?

May 14, 1991

* * * *

Toddler, Cat Interrupt
Mom's Peaceful Nights

Lately, there has been a lot of baby talk surrounding me. Since the family has added two nieces and a nephew and expects a niece or nephew next month, many discussions revolve around car seats, strollers, diapers and sleep schedules.

It is the last topic which seems to garner the most conversation.

Babies are supposed to sleep through the night but they don't.

Most new parents don't mind a baby's sleeplessness during the day, but when it is time to retire for the night they wish the baby had the same agenda. The baby never does. This is his time to howl - literally.

When we talk about 2, 3, 4 and 5 a.m. feedings, I sigh in relief that my children are past that stage.

Usually, I say something like "it is so nice to think that when your

head hits the pillow that's where it will remain until the alarm goes off in the morning."

Unfortunately, my comment lacks credibility. I don't have a tiny baby to keep me awake at night, but I do have a 2-year-old son and a cat whose combined efforts cut into my tranquility.

Matthew likes to keep me from going to bed and the kitty prefers to keep me from staying in bed once I'm there.

My 2-year-old likes to while away the evening hours making a mess of things. I always tell him, "It is a good thing you're so cute because you're so naughty."

His reply, "I'm not naughty," might be spoken as he's mixing spices into paper muffin cups.

When he finally runs out of steam, he says, "I want to sleep in your bed."

"If you do where will I sleep?" I ask. He points to one side of my bed. "What about Dad, where will he sleep?"

"I dunno. On the couch."

As you probably can imagine, his Dad doesn't care for that arrangement so we resort to firm parenting. We say, "You stay in your own bed or there'll be the biggest trouble ever."

This never works, which isn't surprising. You can't blame a little guy for trying to find out what "the biggest trouble ever" will be.

He doesn't find out because we give in and let him sleep in our bed until he falls asleep.

First we have to undergo a thrashing session where Matt kicks the covers off himself, then his Dad and me. Then he kicks us and flops his body around as if he were bouncing on a trampoline. This is the way a 2-year-old sleeps.

It is hard to believe, but I fall asleep during this activity only to wake 45 minutes later after nearly smothering when Matt flips and lands across my face.

I carry him to his bed and just as soon as I am comfortably sinking into oblivion the cat gets up and meows at the side of my bed until I let him outside via my bedroom window.

Most nights the cat gets outside and decides he doesn't like the weather or that he's bored and wants to come back inside. He meows, this time outside the window, until he wakes me and I let him in.

On nights that the weather is mild I leave the window open so the kitty can come and go without my assistance. Although, every time he does, I hear him and I flinch before I look. What if instead of the

kitty coming back a raccoon, a lion or a tiger enters?

So far, none has. But if one did, I probably wouldn't care as long as it was quiet and didn't try to sleep in my bed.

May 15, 1989

* * * *

At the Beep, Leave a Message - And She Does

My voice has been recorded all over town.

I don't think you could call me a recording artist, but I know I have been heard on cassette tapes in numerous households at least once before being erased.

I'm talking about talking to answering machines. I used to dislike answering machines, but I've put those feelings behind me. I've had a change of heart. Now I like answering machines.

I disliked them because I was intimidated by them. I didn't like having a machine-recorded voice answer the phone line when I was making a call because that meant if I wanted to talk, I had to talk to the machine. That didn't bother me too much because I'll talk to anyone - even a machine.

What I didn't like was the idea of my voice being recorded and then broadcast later around a room for anyone to hear. What if a whole room full of people listened? They might think I sound stupid or think I'm a pest for calling and leaving messages.

So, for a long time if an answering machine answered the phone, I would hang up. I always made sure I put the receiver down before I heard the beep, which is the signal to start talking, so the answering machine's owner wouldn't have a clue who called.

If I did get up my courage to leave a message, I'd do it very timidly and nervously. I would become so flustered waiting for the beep that I would blurt out my name, phone number and message before the beep. And then after the beep, I would babble on asking myself if I did it correctly. Just in case, I'd leave my name again to make sure they knew what silly person left the message.

I'm much braver now. I'll talk to anybody's answering machine in a calm, self-assured voice - which means now I wait until after the

beep to start talking.

I still get rattled when I try to remember all the questions I've been instructed by the message to answer. I don't have too much trouble with my name and phone number, but when they ask for the date and time of my call I get really rattled. I need to stop and think and check my watch - and I worry my allotted time will run out. Another suggestion is to leave a short message. What's a short message? I can never say anything in just a few words. So, I talk real fast.

If I have to make a lot of calls, it is nice to get an answering machine if people aren't home. Why? Because my message will be received. Otherwise, I would have to keep calling until someone was home.

The best deal about answering machines is on a long-distance call. If I get a machine, I can leave my message in less than a minute and the call costs less than a postage stamp. If someone is home, there's little chance that I could leave the same message without at least 10 minutes of additional conversation. Of course, if you don't want to talk to a machine, you're stuck with the toll call charge for the connection.

My neighbor said she sang "Happy Birthday" long distance to her granddaughter on her son's answering machine. The little girl was excited to hear her Grandma's voice and she played it over and over again.

I've had a lot of experience with talking into answering machines, but I've never been on the receiving end of an answering machine. I decided I needed to be, so I went over to my neighbor's house to see hers.

I said to Machaela, who was playing in the yard, "I'm going over to Mrs. T's and I want you to call me there."

"Why?" Machaela asked.

"I want to see what it is like to get a call at her house. Her number is written by the phone. Go in the house now and call me."

She looked at me a little strangely, but she went inside and telephoned. I didn't answer.

The answering machine kicked in and Machaela, "a '90's woman" undaunted by technology, left her message: "This is Machaela Cavanaugh from across the street, it is Monday, May 7, 1990 at 5:15 p.m. You know the phone number. My message is: 'You're weird, Mom.'"

May 15, 1990

* * * *

Let Summer Begin!
Mom Is Eager for Change of Pace

A lot of moms will cringe when they read this: I can't wait until school is out.

I'm ready for a change - even if it means wet bathing suits and towels on the furniture.

What we won't have is after-school madness. What goes on between 4 p.m. and early evening is fodder to fell the faint of heart.

Things have to get better now that the soccer season is winding down. Especially after a day like this one:

It began in the early morning when my husband left on a business trip. That left us minus additional driver No. 1.

At 3 p.m., Patrick called to say he would go directly from school to work. (Minus additional driver No. 2 and baby sitter No. 1).

At 3:30 p.m., I remembered that my college helper was not coming to our house that day. (Minus additional driver No. 3 and baby sitter No. 2.)

At 3:50 p.m., I drove Colleen to her job. (Minus baby sitter No. 3.)

At 4:30 p.m., I loaded the whole group into the car to take the girls to dance class. (Minus short-term baby sitters Nos. 4 and 5.)

At 4:45 p.m., I darted into the supermarket and left the four youngest children in the car, supervised by a friend not old enough to baby sit but capable enough to keep the little guys from running through the parking lot after me.

At 5:15 p.m., we stopped at a service station to fill the car with gas and have the vehicle washed.

I pulled into the car wash, the water started pumping and as the brushes began their descent upon my four-wheel-drive vehicle, I realized I forgot to pull in the large side mirrors.

I rolled down the window on the driver's side, pulled in that mirror and repeated the process on the passenger side. The mirrors escaped harm, but my clothes and hair were laundered along with the car.

At 5:40 p.m., I arrived home, dried off, brought the groceries into the house and put them away.

At 5:50 p.m., I ran upstairs to find John's soccer shirt and shinguards because he couldn't find them. I decided to look for Machaela's soccer gear at the same time. By some miracle, I found everything in a matter of seconds.

I rushed downstairs, opened cans of spaghetti and meatballs and

threw the food into the microwave.

At 5:55 p.m., I slopped the spaghetti onto paper plates and herded the troops to the table. They didn't like the meal (I didn't blame them) and wanted to open a box of fun fruits instead, which I let them do.

At 6 p.m., the girls arrived home from dance class. Machaela rushed upstairs to change for the soccer game.

I asked Maureen to stay home with the boys, but she wanted to go to the game because her friend would be there. (Minus baby sitter No. 4 again.)

That meant everyone would tag along. We had to find shirts and shoes for the four little guys, and we had to hurry because we already were late.

John and Machaela's games, of course, were being played at fields miles apart.

After the games, we headed for an end-of-the-season pizza party, which turned out to be a sampling of what hell must be like.

The people and pizza were great, but the place was filled with video games. My pockets were rapidly emptied.

We arrived home after 9 p.m.

Summertime isn't any less hectic. Lawn-mowing replaces snow-shoveling; baseball replaces soccer; swimming lessons replace dance lessons.

But the big difference is that there is no school, so we can spread out the madness.

Life should be easier that way, shouldn't it?

May 22, 1989

* * * *

Custom Cake Makes Big Hit

The graduation cake was enormous. I had it made for the party my husband and I were having with Colleen's friend, Kelly, and her parents, Mark and Susan Laughlin, for all the girls in Colleen and Kelly's graduating class from Marian High School. I ordered the biggest cake I could get and it didn't fit into a box. It had to be set on a slab of cardboard with cardboard pieces taped on to make edges.

The party invitation had caricatures of the two girls, who are both

red-haired, outfitted in caps and gowns and holding a banner that read "Marian High School Class of 1992." It was designed by K.C. Kiner, who is my partner and illustrator for our "Pete" books. She drew up a layout on a board, which I took to a self-service printing shop to make copies on white cards.

After I cut the cards to the right size, I brought the pile home and set my young artists to work. They used colored markers to fill in the red hair, the colored streamers, confetti designs and graduation tassels.

I thought this project would be fun for my children. They said, "You always say that when you want us to do stuff, and it's not true." This reaction surprised me since I said they could watch a "double dose of Danza" (the "Who's the Boss" television show) while they colored.

We finished making the invitations just in time for Kelly and Colleen to give them out at school on the last day of their final exams.

The girls said everyone thought the invitations were cute, so I asked the bakery to duplicate the artwork onto the cake. Next we had to figure out how to transport the oversized cake. I considered having the cake airlifted to the Laughlins' house, with the cake hanging in suspension from the fuselage of the plane, but the landing would have involved cutting a hole in Laughlin's roof to set the cake on their dining-room table.

If the weather weren't threatening rain, we could have had the airplane fly low and set the cake down outside on a picnic table. But I vetoed the plan when I figured renting an airplane would use up all the money saved by not sending the invitations in the mail.

Kelly's sister, Kathleen, came to take me and the cake to their house. We loaded up her car with the other stuff we were taking for the party and then I carried out the cake. It was four layers with filling in between and it weighed approximately the same amount as a three-quarter-ton truck. If you have ever carried a three-quarter-ton truck you'll agree that the cake was heavy. But I have pretty strong arms built up by several years of hauling around three-quarter-ton babies.

Getting the cake into the car was our next hurdle. Kathleen climbed into the back seat to help negotiate the cake into place. It took both of us to lift it up over the front seat and place it securely in back. Then I rode to the Laughlin's hanging on to it just in case it started tipping off the seat.

The cake was a big success at the party, but we barely made a dent in it. After the party was over, it still weighed a half-ton. We brought the cake back to our house to serve at Colleen's graduation open house the next day. Gradually the cake was whittled down in size to fit on a turkey platter.

After all the maneuvering, the frosting was beginning to stick to the sides of the cardboard. But the cake still looked good enough to eat, which I managed to do with gusto until it occurred to me that the cake and I had had a reversal of fortunes. It's loss was my gain literally.

May 26, 1992

* * * *

'Memorial Day Wasn't Place For Miniskirt'

Today is Memorial Day. My grandma always called it "Decoration Day" because she decorated the graves of her relatives.

They were my relatives, too, but we didn't seem related because they died long before I was born.

Grandma always took peonies to the cemetery; she wrapped the flowers in newspaper to keep them from dripping water on the car seat. Whenever I see peonies, I think of Grandma and Memorial Day.

I love peonies - they are big, beautifully colored and always have an ant crawling over the buds, which makes them seem so natural.

When I was a girl, we had a parade down main street on Memorial Day. I always marched with my Girl Scout troop.

The Girl Scouts joined the Boy Scouts, the American Legion, the high school band, the Illinois State Reformatory School marching band (the school is in St. Charles, my hometown), the fire trucks and some of the prominent local residents who rode in convertibles and tossed candy to kids on the curb.

By eighth grade, my friend, Cindy, and I thought we were too cool to march in the parade with all of the little Girl Scouts and Brownies.

We just wanted to go to the cemetery and then to a coffee shop to eat, but our leader insisted that we march in the parade. We grudgingly agreed.

The night before the parade, I slept at Cindy's house. We had a lot

MAY

to do to get ready for the next morning.

We had planned to sew our new badges onto our sashes, but we decided instead to put some pizazz into our parade attire.

First, we shortened our uniform skirts. This was several years before the era of the miniskirt, but we thought the above-the-knee length would be very shocking.

Cindy's skills as a seamstress were better than mine - even though she accidentally kept sewing the skirt to her pajama leg - so while her skirt was only short, mine was short and sloppy. I hemmed my entire skirt with seven or eight very long and uneven stitches.

Our hair was next to fix. We wanted to have really outrageous hairdos, so we inserted brush rollers in all different directions to achieve a wild effect.

The next morning when we showed up at the parade site, the only impression we made was ridiculous.

Our leader looked at us in horror, but all she said was, "Did you stitch that sewing badge on your sash?"

When I told her I had been too busy fixing my hair and hemming my skirt, she was relieved.

She made Cindy and I carry the flag draped in front of us so we would be less conspicuous.

On this holiday weekend, we will take the family to an outdoor memorial Mass and will visit Grandpa Cavanaugh's grave to plant some summer flowers and to say a few prayers.

Memorial Day is a good time to remember peonies, parades, short skirts, wild hair, my grandma and all of our loved ones who no longer are with us.

And it is especially important to honor the men and women who lost their lives protecting the freedoms that we enjoy and celebrate on this holiday and every day.

May 29, 1989

JUNE

June is bunted in by baseball bat as we bask in balmy breezes and bite into bratwurst. Bashful brides and bridegrooms beam blissfully as the best man gives his bleary eyed blessing. A billy goat eats blueberries from a basket and begonias blossom on the back porch.

JUNE

Sunday	Monday	Tuesday	Wednesday	Thursday	Friday	Saturday
			1	2	3	4
5	6	7	8	9	10	11
12	13	14	15	16	17	18
19 Father's Day	20	21	22	23	24	25
26	27	28	29	30		

JUNE

'College World Series Is Educational Adventure'

My husband sometimes asks, "Were you born in America?"

Of course, I tell him. I have a Midwestern accent; I can name the Mouseketeers; I can swing a Hula Hoop.

I think summer vacations should last three months; I display the U.S. flag each holiday, and I know the lyrics to the first verse of the "Star Spangled Banner."

What prompts this man of mine to question my heritage? It's my lack of knowledge about baseball.

As far as he's concerned, a grasp of such terms as fast ball, force out and tag up is fundamental proof of American citizenship.

I plead guilty to ignorance of the finer points of baseball. As my husband points out, it was impossible to grow up in the 1950's and '60s without exposure to the great American pastime. Especially since I grew up in the Chicago area when the Cubs always were on the bottom and the White Sox made it to the World Series.

I even played baseball as a child. I wasn't very good. We had neighborhood games where we chose teams. I usually was chosen last. It never bothered me. I was scared to catch the ball.

I never used a mitt because I'm left-handed and nobody had a left-handed mitt for me to borrow.

I just stood in the outfield, waiting for the other team to make three outs so I could have my turn at bat.

I usually could get a base hit and advance to second base with the help of the next batter. If it was a good hit, I'd try for third base or even home plate.

If there was any more to know about baseball, it went over my head - just like all those fly balls.

Today, I almost have enough knowledge of the game to be a legitimate fan. There are several reasons for my enlightenment.

I've been to three baseball movies in the last couple of years; my children play in Little League; and I've taken in the College World Series.

For years, the series didn't interest me. John took the big kids to the ballpark while I stayed home with the little kids.

One year, John persuaded me to go along. It was fun.

I saw a lot of people I knew, and I didn't need to fix dinner. The kids asked to buy something to eat every inning. By the seventh inning, they were so full they didn't move until they spotted a cotton candy vendor in the stands.

The next morning - as a ploy to get me to return to Rosenblatt Stadium - I got a pitching demonstration.

John demonstrated a fast ball, a curve ball, a knuckle ball and a change up. He briefed me on how the catcher knows what to expect from the pitcher.

The lesson worked. I was curious to see if I could identify the pitches. I went to another game. And I was hooked.

The College World Series is part of our summer schedule.

This year, we had hoped to see the Creighton Bluejays play for the championship. The Bluejays had an exciting, winning season.

We usually pick a team to root for at the College World Serious (that's what my little guys call it).

Our decision can be swayed if we know someone who attends a school which is represented, if we like the style of a particular team's T-shirts and hats, or if we're impressed with the team's playing ability.

There are a lot of things I don't know about baseball. I do know, however, that the College World Series is a great event to have and to support in our hometown.

I hope to see you out at the old ball game.

June 5, 1990

* * * *

A Dream Came True Saturday
. . . Bluejays Fans Find Inspiration

My family attended the College World Series game Saturday. We knew the parking, the lines and the crowds would be a hassle, but I was compelled to be there.

Creighton University's Bluejays were participating. I'm a Creighton graduate, and it's an Omaha team.

We could have stayed home and watched the game on television, but that wasn't good enough. I knew something special was going to happen. And it did.

We wanted to get to Rosenblatt Stadium early but we had to wait for Maureen to finish dress rehearsal for her dance recital at the

Orpheum theater.

As soon as her part was done, she changed from her costume, jumped into the Suburban with the rest of us and we were off.

I thought we wouldn't all get into the stadium because some of our tickets were for general admission, but I was determined to make the effort.

Everything seemed to work out. We got a close parking space on the side of a steep hill where only four-wheel-drive vehicles are allowed to park. I knew having four-wheel drive would pay off someday. The lines weren't too bad either. Pretty soon, we were all situated.

It was one of the most exciting sports moments I've ever experienced. It was symphony and harmony and magic and connection and attachment and enthusiasm and everything else good working together.

It seemed like the Bluejays did everything right. The outfield catches were spectacular. And the double play when a runner is put out on second and the ball is thrown to first before the batter gets there really excites me. That ball travels so fast!

The high spirits in Omaha inspired by Creighton's appearance in the College World Series aren't just about baseball. They're also about dreams coming true, about wanting something to happen and knowing it's possible because you are good enough to have it happen.

And it all came together for Creighton. They made their dream come true.

Omaha has played host to the CWS for 44 years, but we never had a team of our own participate. Omaha fans usually adopt a team or two to follow. My kids usually pledge their allegiance to the team selling the best T-shirts.

That is fun but it doesn't compare to this year. With the Bluejays in the series, it makes me feel like anything is possible.

When we see our own Creighton Bluejays achieve their dream, it seems to become our dream as well. Every fly ball caught, every run batted in, every base stolen, every strike thrown, every hit and catch are symbols of something else.

When we see a play made with the grace, speed and skill that the Bluejays demonstrate, it inspires us to go the distance in our life's work.

Coach Jim Hendry, his team and coaching staff said they were so appreciative of the support of the fans. But it goes both ways. There was so much giving in that ballpark. The crowd was giving its heart to the players, and the players were playing their hearts out for us.

All in all, we Omahans are having a ball - a baseball! Or maybe it's a change up or a fast ball or a knuckle ball.

Thanks for that, Bluejays.

June 4, 1991

* * * *

Omaha Called "Crack in Atlas "

When we lived in Washington D.C., someone asked me where we were from. When I told her, she said "Omaha, that's the crack in the atlas."

Her husband had relatives from here and that was how their family described our River City. Apparently, when you open up an atlas to a map of the world, Omaha is smack in the middle. It is right where the pages are joined together.

I think it is nice to live in the center of the universe.

That must mean everything else in the world revolves around us. All good ideas, all style, all important trends must begin here and radiate outward.

Oh sure, people elsewhere probably would argue that point while extolling the virtues of their hometown as the fashion capital, a financial hub or the think tank of the Western hemisphere. I agree a lot of these places have recognizable virtues. These attributes are apparent, but those climes never will be as centered, as rooted in reality, as in the middle of it all as what originates in the crack of the atlas.

I also suppose others do not look at our geographical situation in such a lofty light. I often get the feeling that these others feel that Omaha's place on the map puts us half-way to somewhere. For example, my Illinois friends and relatives think of Omaha as a stopping point on a drive to Denver and points farther west.

Our house gets a lot of pit-stop traffic. We think it is fun to show visitors around Omaha and dazzle them with our niceness. We make them sorry that they are just passing through. They are impressed every time.

I'm expecting such a traveler today. Our house serves as a way station similar to the camp grounds on the covered wagon trail. Folks pull in looking for a hot bath, a bed, a place to water the horses (since this is the '90s, I direct them to the nearest gas station) before hitting the dusty trail west at sunrise.

It's a pretty easy way to entertain. Tonight's house guest who makes this trip a few times a year is an especially trouble-free guest. She will arrive after we've eaten dinner. I'll offer to fix her a snack, but she'll say she snacked all along the way and she's not hungry. I'll offer a soft drink or a beer but she will have just finished a soda before she arrived.

"A big glass of cold water would taste great," she'll say.

We'll sit up late chatting and looking at pictures and then we'll both go to sleep and she'll be up and ready to go before I have a chance to butter her a piece of toast.

Once in a while, a passing-through-town guest will be here long enough for us to be more hospitable.

My brother-in-law had business here. He flew into town the evening before to have dinner with our family and stay overnight.

The kids were so excited. They decided to fix up his room like a fancy hotel. They put the mint on the bed pillow and folded the end of the toilet paper roll into a point. They also gave him the cordless phone and told him to call on our teen line and ask for "Miz Manager" (one of his young hosts) if he needed any more mints. They even made up a menu so he could order room service for breakfast.

"Pretty snazzy accommodations," he told us, but he shouldn't have been surprised. That's the kind of treatment you get when you are in the crack of the atlas.

June 11, 1991

* * * *

Dictionary Provides Great Word Game

The computer screen was lit up and I was working on a column when the phone rang. It was late, so I didn't think the call would be for me, but no one else seemed to be making advances to pick it up so I lifted the receiver on my desk. Molly Cavanaugh, my niece, was the caller. "Is Colleen home?" she asked.

I told her, "Not yet, she's still at work." Then I asked, "Are you getting ready for your sojourn?"

"What is a sojourn?" she asked.

"That's what you are going on," I said. Molly, who has just finished her second year at New York University, has an exciting summer job lined up out of town. The dictionary was handy, so I looked up the word and read it to her. Sojourn: to live somewhere temporarily, a brief stay or visit.

"I don't think I have ever heard that word before. I'll have to remember to use it sometime," Molly said.

"For your information, in the dictionary, sojourn comes right after the word soiree - an evening social - and right before the word sol - in music, the fifth tone on the diatonic scale. Before soiree comes the word soil."

"Fascinating," Molly responded.

"I'll give you a dollar if you can guess the word that comes before soil," I told her.

Molly made a quick oral scan through the alphabet stopping at "h" and then backing up to "g." Is the word "soggy"? she asked. It was.

I was glad I had left the prize money at $1 instead of the $10 or $100 prize I had thought of offering figuring she'd never guess the word. I started to tell her all the other words on the page. There was solar, solarium, solar-plexus, solar system and a word I didn't know, solecism, which means to speak incorrectly.

"Are you bored, Aunt Kate?" Molly wondered.

"No, not at all, this is interesting," I told her. "Above 'soggy' comes soft-soap, and then a bunch of sodium words including sodium bicarbonate - a fancy way to say baking soda."

The names Socrates, the Athenian philosopher and teacher, and Sodom and Gomorrah, in the Bible, two sinful cities destroyed by fire, also are on this page."

Molly stopped me mid-definition. "Have Colleen call me. Have fun with the dictionary."

The next day I was upstairs when Molly came over to get Colleen. "Hey, Aunt Kate," she yelled up the stairway "I'm here for my dollar." A couple minutes later I wandered into Colleen's room to chat.

"So when do I collect my prize money?" Molly inquired.

"Oh, you don't get it all at once" I told her. "Haven't you ever read how lottery winners collect their money? They receive it over 20 years. So we'll divide your dollar by 20, which means you'll get a nickel a year for twenty years. That will come to you in quarterly payments of 1 1/4 cents every three months."

"Where are you going to get one-fourth pennies?" Molly asked, even though I think she and Colleen weren't paying much attention to me. They were making plans for the evening.

"That's true, 1 1/4-cent payments wouldn't work. I think it would be better for you to receive 1 cent every three months for nine months and then at the end of the year get a balloon payment of 2 cents, which would be beneficial to you because it will be December and extra money always comes in handy at the holidays."

Then the girls said, "Go look up the definition in the dictionary for 'mathematical nut.' It will describe you."

I did, and it comes right after the word maternity: the state the being of a mother. Somehow it all makes sense.

June 2, 1992

* * * *

Kids Can Bank On Imagination
To Fill the Day

They were supposed to be cleaning the bedroom, but imagination got in the way.

The girls were helping (unenthusiastically) John and Mike pick up their bedroom. I told them to make the beds, collect the dirty clothes and pick up the toys.

But while they were picking up toys, they found a wad of play money and decided to play bank.

The bedroom was transformed into Cavanaugh National Bank. They pulled the writing desk away from the wall to use as the teller's table.

Johnny was the head teller, Machaela was president - she had to sign everything - Mike was another teller and Pete and Matt were security guards who stood in the hall outside the bedroom door protecting the bank.

Matt got his job description mixed up because he kept taking money off the teller's desk and running away with it. The others decided that was OK because every bank needs a robber occasionally.

Maureen established herself as the building owner. The bank was only one of her tenants. She also had a ladies' clothing store in my closet and a coin-operated laundry in my laundry room.

That's where I was. I thought I was doing the laundry, but in actuality I was working as a building maid. That position didn't last long. My station in life escalated rapidly when the bank needed a customer.

Johnny came to me as I was folding clothes and said they needed someone to deposit $1 million.

I knew I better look the part of a rich lady so I draped a silk scarf over my T-shirt, slipped on heels, slung an evening bag over my shoulder, dangled some earrings on my ear lobes, stuck on sunglasses, put a stuffed dog under my arm and strutted down the hallway and into the bank.

It was a great feeling to go into a bank - even if it was an imaginary one - to make a deposit instead of a withdrawal.

The building owner had many personal touches on her premises. All along the hallway walls and up the stairs she hung her picture, which was labelled "owner." One picture was from her first birthday party, another was from kindergarten.

She maintains that in business it is important to present a youthful image.

The building also had a Japanese restaurant where the building owner entertained all of her tenants. With the bank president's help, she served tuna fish in paper muffin cups and bagels covered with melted cheese and chopped into pieces.

None of her guests liked the meal. They thought it was dumb that they had to sit on the floor to eat. They preferred to talk about what they would do with all that money if it were real.

Finally it was time for the bank to close. The employees wanted to go outdoors and the bank president and the building owner became perfume demonstrators as they ran through the house handing out perfume samples sprayed on pieces of paper. I returned to the kitchen sink.

And so another day at home passes.

June 5, 1989

* * * *

JUNE

Bickering a Pastime for the Family

"Shut up that shutting up, you varmint you," I heard a mother say to her children. She apparently was quoting the cartoon character, Yosemite Sam, to get her kids to quit telling each other to shut up.

I'm with her. We could use a lot fewer "shut ups" around our house. "Shut up" seems to be sprinkled throughout each conversation.

I'm not saying my children don't get along or don't have an affectionate feeling toward each other. This bickering is a natural and normal interaction between siblings. At least, that's what I try to tell myself.

During the school year they go a couple rounds before school. Usually those fights are related to food and being tired. An example, "What pig hogged all the Apple-Cinnamon Cheerios?" or "That nerd-baby makes us late every morning because he makes Mom put on his shoes."

After school another couple rounds are battled usually over food again or over a television show. But eventually they have to go to bed. They have a couple fights then, too.

It seems as if the end of school is a signal for the real fights to begin. In summer a lot of time for fighting is freed up. The airwaves at our house are filled with not only "shut up" but "brat," "jerk," "idiot" and "I'm going to kill you." When I start hearing these words woven into every conversation - especially when there is some screaming and furniture tipping over involved - it's time for me to start using all my forceful sayings: "Stop it," "I can't stand that bickering," "I'm at my wits' end" or "You're getting on my nerves."

A silent look - saying "So what's new?" - is usually the response to my outbursts.

Housework generates the biggest fights. I think everyone should do their part around the house. My family members have the idea that their part is to make messes throughout the house and that someone else's part (mine) is to clean up. I'm utilizing guilt when I ask whether they think it is right to be watching television (and, of course, fighting about what to watch) while their mother does the jobs they should be doing?

This tirade is usually met with grumbling and new reasons for arguing. I think it is absolutely genetically impossible for a kid to do any job around the house without first pointing out what his brother or sister isn't doing.

"Why do I have to help? That jerk isn't doing anything." The jerk, who is a sibling, responds, "Shut up!"

If I manage to get two of them working, the next episode relates to how the job is being done. Neither party believes the other one is working hard enough or at all.

"You lazy brat, you've only dried one spoon."

"I'm doing more than you. All you've done is blow bubbles into the dishwater."

"Call me crazy but aren't those clean dishes waiting for you to dry? Oh yeah, I forgot you're too stupid to tell the difference between clean and dirty dishes."

"You're crazy, that's for sure, and dumb, too."

"Mom, I'm not going to stay here and be insulted." She stomps off. Usually some door slamming is involved.

After a split second time lapse, the other party also quits working with the logic that, "It's not fair to make me work when that idiot quit."

And so it goes.

A short time after a recent shut-up-a-thon, the group that had been ready to draw blood were companionably playing a game. How nice, I thought, they have learned to forgive and forget, a good quality to embrace. But the peace was short-lived, a few minutes later that embrace turned into a throat hold.

June 16, 1992

* * * *

4-Year-Old Follows Too Closely in Brother's Footsteps

A friend of our oldest son, Patrick, described our youngest son, Matthew, as a "shrinky dink Pat."

Since Matt looks and acts like Patrick, calling him a shrinky dink is a clever comparison. They both have red hair, blue eyes and fair skin. And they seem to be soul mates.

We had Matt baptized on Patrick's 14th birthday. Patrick was godfather for the 1-month-old Matt. This year, Matt wrote in his pre-school scrapbook that when he grows up he wants to be like

Patrick.

Keeping all this in mind, I wasn't surprised when one more similarity occurred in their lives. When Patrick was 3 years old, he developed a hernia. This spring, at the age of 4, Matthew developed a hernia.

I discovered Patrick's when we were at the airport waiting for his dad's plane to arrive. Patrick and Colleen, who was almost 2 years old, passed the time running wild in the baggage-claim area.

In the middle of this adventure, Patrick came and told me that he had a problem. It didn't distress him too much because he continued running around, but I did take him to the doctor the next day.

Matt's hernia was the same as Patrick's. It seemed inevitable. Surgery was scheduled for last Wednesday with Dr. Stephen Raynor at Children's Hospital.

At the time of Patrick's surgery, we were really impressed with how modern medical techniques in 1976 eased the experience. We had heard from people who had undergone similar surgeries 10 or 15 years earlier that it had been much more involved. We checked Pat into the hospital on a Sunday evening, the surgery was performed Monday morning and we checked him out Tuesday morning.

I stayed overnight at the hospital to be with Patrick, but it didn't seem to be any inconvenience at all compared to what it must have been like in the old days.

Now that 1976 visit to Children's Hospital for Patrick's surgery seems like the old days. The hospital has even changed locations, from 45th and Dewey Streets to near 84th and Dodge Streets.

On the day of Matt's surgery, we arrived at the hospital at 6 a.m. and we were home again in time for lunch. We were so proud of Matt because he was such a good boy. He cooperated with the nurses and doctors before his surgery. He got to pick a flavor for his anesthesia, and he chose watermelon because it is summertime.

When it was time, his Dad carried him to the doors of the operating room. We hugged and kissed him, and Matt went bravely into the nurse's arms. Mom and Dad were brave, too, because big brother Patrick told us everything would be fine.

Afterwards, Dr. Raynor came to get us in the waiting room to tell us how well everything went, and the nurses told us how good Matt was and how cute he was. Of course, we already knew that. One of the nurses told Matt that when he was a newborn, she took care of him in the nursery. He said he remembered her, too.

Almost all of our family members attended a preoperation party at the outpatient clinic the evening before so Matt could see where he would be going the next day. At home, we had what his dad called the "Happy Hernia to You" party, when we gave him a "Where's Waldo" puzzle and Okoboji T-shirt.

Matt was quite excited when he found out that going to the hospital means you get lots of presents, cards and cookies from family and friends.

Just like Patrick, Matt has had a rapid recovery. He was playing outside the next day. But he does have an occasional lapse when he lies down on the couch and says, "My operation hurts. Give me some presents."

I think Patrick taught him to say that.

June 18, 1992

* * * *

Bride's Party Fun and Silly

"We can't have a wedding shower and not do anything."

That was my contribution at the meeting at which my sisters-in-law and I were planning a shower for our niece, Kathleen Lucas, who is marrying Tom Comiskey from Milwaukee on August 14.

We had planned the food and decorations. I thought we needed something else.

"We're not putting on any skits," said my daughters, who sat in on the meeting. They also vetoed "silly" shower games.

I reminisced about games I had played at showers. "How about the game where you make teams and each team dresses up one of the guests as a bride using bathroom tissue. It is amazing how creative people can be doing this, although I did have some problems with the paper tearing on the perforated lines."

This idea was immediately nixed by everybody but my sons, who thought it sounded fun - except they wanted to make mummies out of each other.

At my cousin's shower last summer, we played a game that required examining the contents of each woman's purse. For example, the person with the reddest tube of lipstick in her purse would win a prize. I told my sister, who was organizing the games and had told me what the prizes were, that I wanted to win. So they added a category - the person with the longest grocery receipt in her purse. They thought certainly I would have it, but I didn't. I did win, however, for having the most unusual item in my purse, a tray of water color paints.

"Let's not play any games," my daughters suggested. "We can just eat and open presents."

"We can't," I said. "We want Kathleen to know we cared enough about her to do something special at her wedding shower."

They agreed, but said, "Remember, we're not doing any skits."

So when I described my idea to them they said, "That sounds like a skit." I said. "Not at all. It's a fashion show."

We know the design of the wedding gown is a secret, but we didn't think it would hurt for all of Kathleen's cousins to speculate what her wedding gown might look like.

We thought of Kathleen's interests and then created wedding outfits in those styles.

We had a tennis bride, who wore a white tennis dress, a veil fashioned out of a tennis headband and white tulle, and she carried a tennis racquet bouquet. The golf bride wore white knickers that were actually baseball pants, a golf sweater and tulle-wrapped visor as a headpiece. She carried golf clubs with flowers tied on them.

We also had a homemaker bride who wore a white lace apron and babushka and a bathing beauty bride who wore a white swim suit and a bathing cap with a length of tulle shooting out the hole in the top of the cap. She carried a plastic innertube.

Next came a career-woman bride, a cowgirl bride, a young cousin dressed as an Indian princess bridesmaid and a soccer player bride. To carry off each bridal outfit we used several yards of the least expensive tulle we could find and then draped it all over the cousin brides. It was a pretty clever idea, if I do say so.

For each bride's entrance down the stairs, we played some music sort of appropriate for the costume's theme. For the finale, we brought out all the cousin bride models again to pose with the real bride and played the song "Our Love Is Here to Stay." The girls all thought it was silly, but they had fun being silly.

June 22, 1993

* * * *

Mom Does Lights-Out Job to Lower Bill

When our electric bill arrives, I look over the graph on the lower corner. I check to see how much electricity we've used compared with the usage in the same month the previous year. The latest listing is always higher. This drives me crazy.

We are a turned-on family with little prospect of becoming turned off. For example, I just got up to turn off a television. No one was watching it - no one else is even around. Machaela turned it on while she was putting on her shoes to go baby-sitting, and then she left. Maybe she thought I would go in to watch "Green Acres."

Upstairs, there usually are three or four radios playing full blast. It doesn't matter whether there is anyone up there. The radios are usually playing to well-lighted but empty rooms.

I am pretty sure I am the only person who knows where the off buttons are. I can turn off Maureen's radio with my foot and Machaela's with my toe if I'm barefoot, but with Colleen's I have to be careful to not press the wrong button and end up setting the timer on her clock radio to go off with a combination of beeping and music at 3 a.m.

The lights are never out at the Cavanaughs. The big kids are always out, and I would like to be out like a light (you know, asleep), but I have to stay awake until I hear the front door slam and everyone's home. However, I do my waiting in the dark. But just like an all-night truck stop, our house never closes down. The house is lighted up day and night. Even Broadway theaters are dark once in a while.

If I leave a light on to guide my offspring home, I can be sure that light still will be on in the morning and maybe even more lights and a television set will be on.

I tell them it is embarrassing to wake up in the morning and have the front porch light still on. I gives the appearance that someone who was expected home never made it because they are still out "carrying on" or are in jail.

They tell me they don't turn off the lights because they're not sure if they are the last one home. I wonder whether they think Mom and Dad are out. Even though when our children go out for the evening, they take our cars, their dad is usually well-ensconced on the couch reading a book and I am wearing the look of the haggard housewife. But I suppose we could suddenly shift gears and go out partying until past the time when our children get home.

Since I'm not having much luck with the my energy-conserving

JUNE

lights-out campaign, even though I am dealing with an environmentally aware group that would make me face a firing squad if I brought anything Styrofoam into the house, I'm trying to cut down on electricity use other places.

Instead of always using the clothes dryer, I hang up or lay out to dry as many of the clothes as I can. Having enough room to dry the clothes is my biggest problem. I put up on hangers all the T-shirts, sweat shirts, and regular shirts on a shower curtain pole. I have a drying rack for shorts and jeans and other stuff. I string unmentionables between the knobs on the cabinets over the washer and dryer and I drape bed sheets over the doors.

Sometimes there is so much laundry that it would never dry if it were all jammed together. So I space the hangers out by hanging them along the laundry room molding. As I work, I daydream about how neat it would be to have an outdoor clothesline.

While all the clothes are drying, I go frequently to the laundry room to smooth out the wrinkles in the pants and admire how nicely the shirts are drying. It's fun. My kids tell me I need to get a life. Maybe I do.

Tonight it will be my turn to be the last one to come in. I'll check my laundry and then turn out all the lights. What a night it will be.

June 23, 1992

* * * *

Travelers Get to Know
Hong Kong Transportation System

I just returned from a great adventure. We went to Hong Kong to visit the Tim Finnigans, who used to be our neighbors in Omaha but now live in Hong Kong.

Tim works for United Parcel Service, and his job took him to Asia. His wife is Cindi and their children are Joe, 13, a former classmate of my daughter, Maureen; Ellen, 12, and a bosom buddy of my daughter, Machaela; and Tom, who is 10.

My traveling companions included my son, Patrick, who recently graduated from high school, and Maureen and Machaela.

My husband, John, whose frequent-flier miles accumulated through his business travel enabled us to get our plane tickets, wasn't able to go along, nor was Colleen, who already had made some exciting summer plans when we decided to make this trip.

The Finnigans did everything possible to make sure we had a wonderful time. There is so much to tell. It was such an interesting and fascinating place, and Cindi made sure we saw it all. She was our excellent tour guide.

On our way to the airport to catch our plane home we started adding up the different means of transportation we had used during our stay.

We counted many different forms. Some were conventional ways of traveling; some were quite unexpected and unusual.

Cindi met us at the airport with a car and driver she hired to transport us to her family's apartment.

After our 14-hour plane ride from San Francisco it was awfully nice to have that luxury. The next day we traveled on transportation forms 3, 4, 5, 6, 7 and 8 (numbers 1 and 2 were the airplane and the limo).

We took the shuttle bus (which runs down the hill from the Finnigans' apartment building, which has a spectacular view of Repulse Bay) to the bus stop where we boarded a double-decker bus which took us to Central, the city's center, where we boarded an open-air double-decker bus.

Of course, we rode on top. The bus took us to The Peak tramway, which scaled the side of a big hill to the top of The Peak where we could look out over all of Hong Kong and the surrounding islands.

Our day continued with more sightseeing, shopping (which is the major tourist activity in Hong Kong because of the bargain prices) and more bus riding, including a ride on a double-decker trolley car.

That evening we rode by taxi to a restaurant, which was a welcome change after traveling about all day in a body that said it was Wednesday in a city that said it was Thursday. Jet lag was setting in.

The next day we tried out the MTR, Hong Kong's mass transit railway system. The MTR travels under the bay to Kowloon Peninsula where we went to meet Mr. Lee, an 86-year-old doll maker.

Before he showed us his dolls, he entertained us with stories about his life as the only Chinese teacher 50 years ago in an American school in Shanghai. He also talked of Chinese life and customs.

Transportation forms 8, 9 and 10 were the most memorable. The Finnigans planned for us, their family and two other families an all-

JUNE

day boat trip on a junk, which is a Chinese or Japanese ship made from teak logs.

We would cruise from island to island seeing the sights, then anchor at Lantau Island for swimming off the junk at a secluded beach.

The weather did not cooperate. It rained intermittently. The choppy water made the boat rock and made me seasick. I wasn't alone. Maureen joined me in misery.

When we arrived at Lantau Island we were the first ones to jump onto the sampan, a very small boat. The driver of the sampan charges a small sum to ferry passengers from their junks to the shore, the place I longed to be.

After a rest on the beach and a swim in the South China Sea, I recovered in time to troop through some rice paddies to the remote island restaurant.

By the time we headed back to the junk enough time had elapsed for me to convince myself that I wouldn't get seasick again.

And I didn't. I was too terrified. Twenty minutes into our journey, the waves were lapping at the boat's deck and the wind was blowing all our stuff around.

The boat's driver said he was turning back to the nearest island. We ended up taking the Hong Kong ferry (transportation form number 10) back to Hong Kong. The next day we read in the newspaper that we had been touched by Typhoon Nathan.

The following day we traveled by the Finnigans' car (number 11). The Finnigans don't use their car very often because there aren't many parking places in Hong Kong. It is simpler to use public transportation, which is convenient and inexpensive.

Number 12 was a different ferry to Lantau Island to see the Po Lin Monastery and the largest Buddha in the world. Number 13 was the overpacked, gear-stripping, transmission-dropping bus ride from the ferry to the Buddha.

Number 14 was the island taxi we took to avoid another bus ride.

In Tai O, a fishing village, we took a barge (number 15) across a small canal. It was powered by two elderly women who do their shuttling by pulling a clothes line strung across the canal.

Number 16 was the Star Ferry, which crosses from Hong Kong island to Kowloon peninsula.

Number 17 was the Hovercraft Patrick and I took for our one-day trip to mainland China. In Shozou, China, we boarded a motor coach (number 18) for our trip through Dongguan and onto to Guangzhou, formerly known as Canton.

Our return trip to Hong Kong was made by train (number 19). Elevators (20), escalators (21), stairs (22) and walking (23) bring us to the total number.

June 26, 1990

* * * *

Two Girls' Trip Is No Vacation
For Their Mom

The plane made it. I checked with the airline. Right now I'm waiting to hear if my girls were on it.

My 10- and 12-year-old daughters were beside themselves with excitement by the time they left for New Jersey this morning. They will visit their cousins, my sister and brother-in-law for a week.

For several years, Maureen and Machaela had planned with cousin Megan to make this journey. We finally decided to let them go when there was a good air fare.

Since we made that decision, there has been talk of little else. Maureen had the departure time figured out to the number of minutes for the past four weeks and every day she would update her timetable on her calendar.

Letters crossed in the mail. Megan wrote of all the things they were going to do and Maureen wrote back about what she planned to wear on each of these occasions.

Machaela, who is the youngest of this trio, also wrote to Megan and to Megan's friend who is Machaela's age.

Maureen said she needed money for her trip. Megan had written that they'd be going to New York City for a day. According to Maureen, there is a lot of stuff to buy in New York City.

She took babysitting jobs but she didn't feel that this would garner enough income.

I told her, "You can work for me and I'll pay you."

"Not a good idea," she said. "I already work for you and don't get paid. Whenever I ask to be paid for a job you tell me either I should do the job to contribute my share to the family or that I'm earning my keep."

That's true, I said, "but only because it is such an effort to get anything done. If you work for me without griping, act responsible and do a good job, I'll pay."

And she did. Money is a great motivator.

Machaela was supposed to be in on this money-making venture, but she never got enthused about it. I think she was gambling that I would come up with the spending money even if she never did the dishes without being told.

She was right. But I think she was a bit nervous when Maureen presented me with her total because Machaela began complaining that all she earned was $3 from one babysitting job and someone had taken it.

Soon after the plane reservations were made, the girls discovered that nothing in their present wardrobe was acceptable travel attire.

This meant going on a shopping trip.

I suggest saving their money for shopping during their trip. Maureen responded, "We are saving our money. We'll use your money to get new clothes for the trip."

I felt a strain on my checkbook.

I did want the girls to look nice for the trip, but perhaps not as nice as they wanted to look.

The thought of being away from their home and their parents didn't bother the girls at all. But the idea of changing planes at O'Hare Airport in Chicago did. They had been there and they didn't like the lay of the land.

"We won't know what to do. We'll never find our departing gate. We'll get lost."

We discussed the plane-changing procedure. Then we discussed it again. Even a map of the airport terminal didn't make a dent in their fear level. We opted for an escorted trip. An airline employee would accompany them to and from the gates.

The phone call just came. Maureen and Machaela arrived safely. They are having pizza in my sister's kitchen.

. Their good times have begun.

June 26, 1989

* * * *

JULY

July snares the sunlight. Scorching heat sears the strongest saplings. Swimming is sensational until the sunburn sizzles your skin. On the fourth strike up the band as a summons to show the stars and stripes. Strawberry shortcake satisfies the sweet tooth. Slip into a sarong on a Sunday to sip seltzer in the shade by the lake.

JULY

Sunday	Monday	Tuesday	Wednesday	Thursday	Friday	Saturday
					1	2
3	4 Independence Day	5	6	7	8	9
10	11	12	13	14	15	16
17	18	19	20	21	22	23
24 / 31	25	26	27	28	29	30

JULY

Friends Share July Fourth Favorites
...The Simplest Pleasures
Are the Greatest

It would be difficult not to be aware of Independence Day this week. Everywhere you turn, there is evidence of preparations for a big celebration.

There's every imaginable type of patriotic merchandise on the market. I bought my little guys some red, white and blue shirts at a sidewalk sale. I also purchased a new flag since our old one was worn from being flown during the Persian Gulf war.

I think of the Fourth as a "people holiday," so I decided I'd ask people what they like about the holiday. My survey was random - I just asked whomever happened to call or come by our house.

Sara Knutson, 16: I'm always at camp for the Fourth. (She's a counselor at Camp Kitaki). Around the campfire, we sing "Proud to Be an American" and everyone feels good about our country. It's also the day after my birthday and I get lots of presents.

My niece, Molly Cavanaugh, 18: I like coming over to your house for the family get-together. There's lots of food, we get to use paper plates so there are not as many dishes as usual, and we get to eat Aunt Cathie's watermelon-filled ice cream.

J.T. Boehm, 16: I like the fireworks and corn on the cob.

Spencer Hestwood, 16: I like the Fourth because it's the birthday of our country. It's a great country because I get to go biking from Crested Butte to Aspen, Colorado.

Susan Laughlin, a grown-up: The Fourth of July is a time to go home to northern Wisconsin and visit my family. All the cousins and aunts and uncles gather to celebrate. There's a boat parade on the lake. All the boats are decorated patriotically.

Machaela Cavanaugh, 12: I like swimming with the whole family and eating Aunt Cathie's sherbet watermelon.

The Cavanaugh boys: We like the fireworks and Aunt Cathie's flag cupcakes. Pete, 6, really likes watermelon.

Carlee, 9, Annie, 6, and Joe Sodoro, 4: We like swimming, fireworks, parades, and going on a boat ride.

John Green, a grown-up: I like to get up on the Fourth, play a John Philip Sousa record and put up the flag.

Michelle Gaver, 18: It's my dad's birthday and he thinks it's neat because everyone celebrates it.

Peg and Blain Butner, who were visiting us from Arlington, Virginia: Our neighborhood association organizes a parade. The kids decorate bikes and wear costumes. Afterward, there's a big hot dog and watermelon feed at the community center.

Brian Harr, 19: I like hamburgers on the grill and fireworks.

Burke Harr, 19: I like family get-togethers, watermelon and fireworks.

Judy Schweikart, a grown-up: I like Cathie Amdor's Jell-O molds. She decorates them to look like the flag.

Colleen Cavanaugh, 17: Who always makes those good brownies? I like them.

The simplest pleasures are the greatest pleasures. I agree that watermelon, fireworks and Aunt Cathie's cooking make up a fine celebration for our nation's birthday.

I think that is how our forefathers intended life in America to be.

July 2, 1991

* * * *

Tooth Fairy Does Her Deed In Nick of Time

Mike lost his first tooth. He had been wiggling it when it finally gave way.

Mike and his entourage ran upstairs from the basement to tell me all about it. Everyone was excited.

We needed to find something in which to put the tooth. A little boy's tooth is so small it easily could get lost on the kitchen counter.

Mark John, a visiting buddy, said, "At our house, we always put our teeth in an envelope."

"Why didn't I think of that?" I answered and ran off to find one.

Mike is 6 years old and has known about the tooth fairy for a long time, but he has never had a visit from her. This was an exciting time.

Mike always is angling for ways to get his hands on money. So far, he has been able to earn money only by picking up toys in the basement or doing other chores he doesn't like.

Losing teeth seemed like a much easier way to accrue assets. When his tooth loosened, you almost could see the quarter signs in his eyes.

After we put the tooth in an envelope, I remembered that we had a tooth fairy pillow. It is a little pillow with a pocket to hold teeth.

A child is to place a tooth in the pocket and put the little pillow underneath his bed pillow to await the arrival of the tooth fairy.

I thought the tooth fairy pillow was a cute and clever idea when I received it as a gift, but the pillow was lost in the depths of our toy box before any of the kids lost a tooth.

I think Barbie used the pillow as a mattress in her Dream House.

Mike's tooth was safe in the envelope and he could not have been happier. Anticipation surrounded him when he took the tooth to his bedroom and placed it under his pillow.

The next morning, Mike checked under his pillow and discovered the tooth instead of the money he was hoping to receive. Mike was disappointed but not as disappointed as his mother.

How could I have forgotten to alert the tooth fairy?

"Sometimes the tooth fairy has so many stops, she can't get to them all the first night," I told Mike. "You have to be patient and put your tooth under the pillow again tonight."

To my relief, he accepted this theory.

The tooth fairy promised she would do better the next night, but she didn't.

Mike's tooth was forgotten until, when I was straightening Mike's bed, I discovered the envelope.

Mike, luckily, was downstairs.

I decided if the tooth fairy couldn't come through, I would have to take action.

I checked the hallway and found the coast was clear. I grabbed the envelope and dashed to my room, where I stashed the tooth in my bureau drawer.

I rummaged through a mug of coins that I collect from pockets at laundry time. I found a bunch of quarters, so I let the tooth fairy be generous to make up for her tardiness.

I slipped the money under Mike's pillow.

Then I summoned Mike.

"Did you check to see if the fairy came?" I asked.

"Yes, but she didn't," he said.

"Really? Well, she must have been running late and came while we were eating breakfast because when I was making your bed, I found something. Come and see."

"Wow," Mike said when he saw what was in the envelope. "Four

quarters. How much is that?"

When I told him, he asked, "Do you have a real dollar in your purse to trade me?"

The next day, Mike saw an ad for a toy he wants. The toy costs $6.99.

He figures at $1 a tooth, he only needs to lose his bottom row of teeth and he can get the toy.

July 3, 1989

* * * *

A Task to Be Shared
. . . Mom Delegates Dishwashing Duty

My first summer job was washing dishes.

Whenever anyone inquired about my summer employment, I would say I was "kitchen help." I figured they would think I was the pastry chef's apprentice or the cook's assistant instead of a dishwasher.

At the time, I felt embarrassed to have what I considered a lowly job. I can't say that dishwashing is something I've aspired to do as my life's work - although some days it seems like it is - but it is something I was good at doing. I still am.

I grew up washing dishes. I washed dishes at home, at my friends' houses, in the church hall, at family parties at our house and anywhere else where there were dirty dishes and my mother was in attendance.

It was a joke among my sisters and me - my brothers never did dishes; apparently, they were exempt because they took out the garbage once in a while - that we would wash dishes at our weddings. None of us did.

However, I did end up in the kitchen at one of my wedding showers. At my mother's prodding, Margie Johnson - my friend who also grew up with dishpan hands - and I were instructed in the middle of the festivities to "get some of the punch glasses and dessert plates cleaned up."

As we bent over the dishwasher, dressed in our party garb, Margie said to me, "How come we always end up here?"

In addition to learning at my mother's sink how to scrape, stack, scrub and squirt suds, I also figured out how to get others involved in the job.

My children claim I have learned this too well.

I always tell whoever happens to be near my sink that as Father Mac (my pastor, the Reverend A.J. McMahon at St. Joan of Arc) says, "It doesn't matter who does the work as long as the work gets done." Dishes are usually the work I want done.

"Washing dishes elevates your status," I tell my children and their friends.

"How so?" they ask skeptically, as if I would make something like that up.

"Well, if you wash dishes for me or at someone else's home, we are bound to have a higher opinion of you than if you just came into the house, hung around eating our ice-cream bars, and never pitched in and helped with the tidying up when it needed doing."

It is important when you are a teen-ager to be held in high esteem by your friends' parents. Visualize this scene: A group of parents are talking about a certain individual who was seen fleeing from the police, going 120 miles per hour in a stolen beer truck after holding up a taco stand, a video store and a cigarette salesman.

If I was involved in the conversation, I could interject that it wasn't possible for that young person to have been on such a joy ride because he or she was at our house washing out the broiler pan. That type of person never would blow soapsuds in the face of law and order.

If that situation isn't a worry, consider another benefit from washing dishes - clean fingernails.

I may be the champion dish-washing instigator, but the actual "kitchen help" title would have to go to two of my sisters-in-law, Mary Anne Lucas and Pat Cavanaugh. No one could come close to the number of times they have stuck their hands into my dish water.

They say that's why I invite them to parties. Which isn't true at all.

I ask Mary Anne because she brings her layered salad and Pat because she makes good cheese potatoes.

July 9, 1991

Family Gets to the Bottom of Half-Filled Pops

Our Fourth of July party left our house in a shambles, but it was a good shambles because it was proof that we'd had a good time.

We made a couple stabs at straightening up before going to bed but decided that the task was overwhelming. We put all the food away and left the debris until morning.

Unfortunately, the good fairies didn't come in while we were asleep to tidy up. The mess still was there facing us the next day. My course of action was to get the troops mobilized. I was at command central - the kitchen sink - and everyone was to report to me.

Johnny wanted to know why he and his brothers had to do back-breaking work (picking up papers and toys in the yard) while his sisters were sitting down eating leftover taco dip. Good question. The girls said they were recovering from washing the dishes.

Their dad was cleaning up on the deck and patio. After a bit he came back into the house holding a recycling bag filled with aluminum cans.

"I emptied 15 half-filled pop cans," he told me. "What those kids must do is take a can of soda pop, open it up, take a couple swigs and put it down. Then the next time they want a drink they open up another can and then leave that one sitting somewhere.

"I think that's exactly what happens." I told him.

"That's wasteful," he told the girls, who still were hard at work eating the taco dip.

At first the girls didn't react, but when their dad pressed the issue they looked up and defended themselves.

"It wasn't me. I only had one can of pop all day and I finished it." Machaela said.

"Me neither. I was drinking Kool-Aid," Maureen told him.

"Don't look at me," I said. "I was drinking ice water."

"How come I saw you opening a bottle of wine?" asked Mike, who had come inside because he thought he felt raindrops. "Didn't you drink that?"

"OK, I had some wine at dinner, but that comes in a bottle, not an aluminum can," I said. "But you are half-right. I didn't drink the whole bottle of wine, I even shared it with other people and then I left the half-finished bottle on the counter.

When John went back outside to empty some more half-filled pop cans the girls asked me, "Do you think Dad wants us to call everyone from the party and tell them to come back over and finish drinking their pop?"

"No," I answered. "But that's not a bad idea because then they could eat up some of these leftovers and I can get the refrigerator cleaned out."

I think opened and then-neglected pop cans are a fact of summer. Being able to dig into a cooler filled with ice-cold cans of pop adds to the festivities at a summer picnic.

Of course, my family doesn't need the pop to be ice cold. They just like the idea of having their own can. The day before the party my husband bought a case of Sprite. Later, when he came inside the house looking for a cold drink after working in the yard, he found an empty Sprite box and opened and half-drunk green cans littering the kitchen counter.

It was kind of a discouraging scene, but it shouldn't have been. After all, a case of Sprite doesn't disappear like that every day. For example, today it was a twelve pack of Coke that vanished. And tomorrow it will be glasses of water all around.

July 14, 1992

* * * *

Pilots Create First-Class Memories

As I write this, I'm flying first class from Omaha to Chicago.

The reason I'm flying first class instead of coach, as is my custom, is that my brother, Billy, is the co-pilot. He bumped my husband and me up to first class.

This elevation in status means we get to drink our orange juice from real glasses instead of plastic ones and there's extra leg room, a nice amenity.

This is fun. It is nice to have a blood relative in charge of ferrying me through the skies. When we boarded the plane, Billy took us into the cockpit to see the instruments and to meet the rest of the crew. They looked like they knew what they were doing, which made me feel good.

That we happened to be on Billy's plane was a coincidence. In a recent phone conversation, he asked if we were busy Wednesday night because he had a layover in Omaha and would like to see us - or, more correctly, to see his nieces and nephews.

I said we would be home but we were leaving the next morning, possibly on his flight.

Even though we were going to the airport for the same early morning flight, Billy didn't think it wise to stay at our house overnight. He thought it more prudent to return to the hotel after dinner to stay with the rest of the flight crew.

I told him we could get him to the airport on time, but he thought better of this plan. He was correct not to trust us because I had a selfish motive. I thought if we had the co-pilot with us, the chances of the plane departing without us would be diminished.

Billy said he needed to be at the airport earlier than our customary last-second arrival. He's familiar with the way we operate.

For example, why get to the airport 45 minutes before the plane is scheduled to depart when we could spend that 45 minutes asleep at home?

After all, we need that extra rest so we are fit to run through the airport, cut in line at the security check and arrive out of breath at the gate seconds before the jetway is pulled back.

This is not the only time I've had a relative in the cockpit. The first time I flew on an airplane, my father was the captain. My mother, sister and I flew to Washington, D.C., out of Chicago's Midway airport with two stops in Ohio - Dayton and Cleveland.

My sister, Bonnie, was 10 years old; I was a year younger. We checked out the ladies rooms in all of these airports.

When we arrived in Washington, a purser for the airline greeted our plane and startled my sister by giving her a big kiss. I was able to duck in time - he missed my cheek and kissed the air.

Since we were relatives of the pilot, we rode first class. We got to eat all the extra desserts - individual pumpkin pies.

On the return trip, we had to circle Chicago for an extra hour before we could land. My stomach's reaction to the combination of too much pie and the long air trip shouldn't be used as a testimonial to my father's flying.

Nevertheless, I remember that trip as a highlight of my childhood.

How does my father's namesake compare in flight to my Dad? I say great. I'll give him a very good grade, and I wouldn't even mind if he has someone at the gate to greet me with a big kiss.

July 17, 1990

* * * *

Gores, Convention Leave Many Memories

I hadn't planned to go to the Democratic National Convention in New York City. My husband, who is more involved in political events than I am, was to be out of the country for a business trip. My plan was to observe the convention via CNN and the network news programs.

Then the drama for the selection of the vice presidential nominee unfolded.

"What if our own Bob Kerrey gets the nod?" I thought. "It would sure be a thrill to be in New York to see it."

But Kerrey was not to be the candidate this time. Senator Al Gore of Tennessee was picked.

Al and my husband, John, went to Congress together in 1976. Al and his wife, Tipper, became good friends of ours. We shared many good times as couples and with our families.

We celebrated New Year's Eve 1978 together in the Washington home of another congressional couple because Tipper and I were both too pregnant to travel back to our home states for the holidays. I think her due date was December 31 and mine was a couple days later. Tipper and I kept each other's spirits up as we waited to give birth to our beautiful daughters, Sara for her and Machaela for me.

Over the years in Washington we shared birthdays, holidays when we were both in Washington and numerous public events. Since my family moved back to Nebraska, we have kept up our friendship with the Gores and have exchanged visits to Nebraska and Tennessee.

It seemed a shame that John and I weren't going to participate in the festivities. Then the phone rang and my plans changed. Judy Schweikart, a friend and a delegate to the convention, was on the line.

"Kate, I think you should come to the convention even though John isn't able to attend."

I hemmed and hawed, citing stumbling blocks that would prevent me from going, but Judy persisted with solutions.

"The Nebraska delegation will include you in the events and arrange passes to Madison Square Garden. Jim Cavanaugh (my brother-in-law) will be there, and haven't you already received invitations from the Gores?"

By the end of the phone call I told Judy yes and by the end of the evening my two oldest children, Patrick and Colleen, had also figured

out how they could go, too.

Patrick's friend, Burke Harr, who had just finished a summer internship in Senator J.J. Exon's Washington, D.C., office, joined us in New York City. I wondered whether these college kids felt their style was cramped having "Mom" along but if they did they didn't let on.

In New York at the St. Regis Hotel we attended a brunch for the Nebraska delegation. The event's hosts were Ted Sorensen, a Nebraska native who was President Kennedy's speech writer, and his wife, Gillian. Also attending was another Nebraska native, Dick Cavett.

It seemed like everywhere we went we were able to get pictures taken with someone famous. Then we lost the camera. Luckily, we often were with Jim Cavanaugh and our friend, Mary Barrett, who both were snapping lots of photos.

So we don't have all of our pictures, but we do have great memories - especially of the last night of the convention when Clinton and Gore made their acceptance speeches. It was very exciting.

July 21, 1992

* * * *

Teen Son Suits Himself
But Learns to Be Thrifty

In case you might wonder, today's column was written with permission from my son, Patrick. He is indifferent about his appearance.

When Patrick went off to college last year, I filled a garment bag with his high school graduation clothes: sport coat, slacks, shirt, shoes, socks and tie. The clothes were clean, pressed and ready to wear whenever he needed them - although he doubted he would ever need to look that nice.

At Christmastime, I told him to bring home his good clothes because he would have to dress up for a few holiday occasions.

He lost the sport coat at the first special event at home. Of course, I didn't realize it until the day of the second special event.

Somehow, he made it through that event and through the rest of the school year dressed not quite as his mom would have liked, but good enough to suit himself.

I didn't think about his lack of dress clothes until this summer, when we had a wedding to attend. Patrick didn't concern himself with what he would wear - I guess he thought why bother when he has me as his personal valet.

The day before the wedding, I purchased a sport coat for him - with his approval. I didn't particularly like the jacket, but the price tag was tolerable.

I was still grieving over the lost sport coat when I started searching Patrick's room for his dress shoes. As it turned out, he had left them at school.

That was a problem. Even if I had been willing to buy another pair, our mission would have been difficult. Patrick's shoe size isn't readily available. We had to special-order his last pair, and there wasn't time to do that again.

We couldn't even borrow a pair because no one we knew shared Patrick's shoe size.

Then I got an idea. Another mother in a similar situation went to a thrift store.

That afternoon, when Patrick got home from his summer job, he took 10 seconds to try on his new clothes. He said they were fine. Then I told him we were going to a Goodwill store to look for shoes. He agreed, reluctantly.

He said he could just wear any old shoes. I was afraid he might have to - until we got lucky.

While we were at the Goodwill store, I suggested looking at the sport coats. We found one similar to the one I had bought for almost 20 times the money earlier in the day.

The jacket, which fit Patrick, even had a designer label. Then we walked over to the shoe section. I picked up a pair of very nice men's dress shoes - like the ones my son had left at school. "Try these," I told Patrick. They fit.

I was thrilled. The shoes were $2.99. I wondered aloud why someone would practically give away such a good pair of shoes.

Patrick said, "Maybe the guy who owned them is dead."

"Maybe," I agreed. "But I bet he'd be happy to know his shoes will be out dancing at a wedding reception tomorrow."

When we got home, I put the sport coats side by side on the couch and had everyone try to guess which was which. My family couldn't tell the difference. I think they were making fun of me, but I didn't care.

The day after the wedding, a bag of clothes appeared on our front porch. The boys found some shorts to try on; a friend of Patrick's found a pair of pants he says he wears to work every day. The girls were turning the jeans into cutoffs before I figured out that the clothes came from a friend who had been cleaning closets.

In another era, these "new to them" clothes would have been called hand-me-downs. But in the '90s, that stigma is gone. My children are wearing recyclables.

July 23, 1991

* * *

Mom Knows Better,
but She's Having a Rash of Problems

The weeds of summer have given me problems - a next of skin sort of trouble.

I have poison ivy. I have never had it before and I've decided I never want to have it again. Although, the way it seems now, I may never have the chance to get a new case because I'll never get rid of this case.

When I was a kid, I thought it would be neat to get poison ivy. On Girl Scout outings, I'd look for it when we went on plant-identifying hikes. I don't ever remember seeing it; I was disappointed.

I figured it couldn't be that bad to have - plus I'd get a lot of attention if I got it accidentally on purpose. Whenever characters in the movies got poison ivy, it was always a comedy scene, which looked like fun.

My recent predicament has shattered that childhood illusion. I think I got my poison ivy when we went on a hike along the Platte River. At first, I only had it on the back of my knee, but now it has spread to the far corners of my bumpy, itching body. I've got it on my other knee, arms, elbows, neck and in places that wouldn't be on display unless I was posing for the Sports Illustrated swimsuit edition.

This is a real itchy deal. Luckily, I have long enough fingernails for scratching. If one of my children had poison ivy, I'd be after them not to scratch - but I have to scratch. If I couldn't scratch, I would have to find a gravel road and roll around in it.

The itching is worst at night. I usually have to get out of bed to put on my calamine lotion, but I'm not sure it does much good since it's so runny. One night when I was trying to put it on my knee - in the dark - I spilled it all over the sheets. So I just got back into bed and set my leg on the calamine spot.

The next night, to avoid another spill, I decided to use an applicator. Once again it was dark, so I grabbed what I thought was a washcloth. Instead, it was a pair of underpants from the laundry basket full of clean clothes. Now the underpants are calamine-lotion pink. Luckily, pink is one of my favorite colors.

Since my breakout, I have been suspicious of any type of vegetation. What if I didn't get the poison ivy on our hike? What if I got the rash from walking along the sidewalk next to the petunias or when I watered the geraniums?

Finally, on a day when I wasn't itching much, I decided to be brave and tackle the weeds which seemed to be overtaking our garden. I got my daughters and their friend, Kristine, away from the telephone and television to help me. We were working hard making some headway with the weeds when I suddenly ran screaming out of the garden.

Maureen said she thought I'd seen a mouse, but it was worse than that. I had disrupted a hornet's nest and several of the tenants were on me - stinging their lives away. Just as many were on the dog, who was right beside me in the garden, and lots more were buzzing around trying to find a target. All of them were as mad as hornets can be. We all ran into the house as fast we could.

I couldn't figure out if my reaction to this new outdoor episode was emotional, physical or if I just felt weird because I was already covered with red blotches and now I had a bunch of new ones. Or maybe it was the after effects of the Ultra Slimfast shake I had for breakfast.

But there is a happy ending to this story. My girls are finishing the weeding project. They think I should stay away from weeds for awhile. At least until I get the itch to scratch again.

July 30. 1991

* * * *

Little Redheads Succeed at Shocking Mom

The phone conversation was progressing smoothly. I was talking with a committee chairman about my responsibilities for a charity.

As we spoke, I paced around my kitchen fixing our evening meal and making mental notes.

As I made a pass by the refrigerator, I could see the driveway.

"Oh, my goodness!" I shrieked.

The woman on the other end of the telephone, I'm sure, didn't know what to think. So I quickly explained that my four young sons had just returned from the barbershop, where they had had their hair cut "boot camp" style. Each one was balder than the next.

As they lined up in front of me in the kitchen, they were all smiles. They had provoked the exact reaction from their mom that they had hoped for. I was stunned.

"What happened to your hair?" I asked, which was a dumb thing to say because it was obvious that they had been sheared like sheep.

"You all look like it's 1955 again and you're in style. Or else it's 1968 and I'm experiencing deja vu - seeing your dad in quintuplet right after he joined the Army."

The boys had been taken to the barbershop by our baby sitter, Campbell. The guys were looking a bit ragged, so she offered to take them for a trim.

"Getting our hair buzzed was all Chewy's idea," Pete told me.

"Oh, really?" I answered.

It seems that Chewy, being the youngest, was the last to get into the barber's chair. The other fellows' hair already was conservatively trimmed.

"I want a flat top like Bart Simpson's" he told the barber.

The barber looked to Campbell for permission.

"I'm not their mother, but I guess it will be OK." She was thinking, "I can handle the mother," which she did by appealing to my pocketbook.

She told me later, "You always say you wish the boys wouldn't have to have their hair cut so often because it costs so much. I figured these haircuts would save you a couple of trips."

When the other three saw what was happening, they had to have their hair cut the same. The barber gladly obliged and let the other three back into the chair. When he was finished, there was a load of red hair on the floor.

The result must have been trendsetting, because a fellow with a 60s' style ponytail told the barber he wanted a flat top, too.

I'm finally getting used to looking at the boys' scalps. Of course, I'd think they were cute no matter how they wore their hair.

In addition to the savings, there are other benefits to the short cuts. The boys are cool, and they don't need a comb or much shampoo.

There's not much I can do about my four fuzzy-headed guys except be grateful that the girls weren't along.

July 31, 1990

AUGUST

August alludes to days of acclaim. On the second,
our wedding anniversary, allurement is in the air
and amber accessories are apparent. On the first
and the twenty-second the afternoon ague
ascends when the ambrosia of birthday cake
alights into the atmosphere. Along the fence
asters have acquired an assemblage of colors.

AUGUST

Sunday	Monday	Tuesday	Wednesday	Thursday	Friday	Saturday
	1 *JOHN'S BIRTHDAY*	2 *OUR ANNIVERSARY* ♡	3	4	5	6
7	8	9	10	11	12	13
14	15	16	17	18	19	20
21	22 *MATT'S BIRTHDAY*	23	24	25	26	27
28	29	30	31			

AUGUST

Something Is in the Air In Europe

When I prepare for any kind of gathering at our home, I get out all sorts of things: the ice bucket, flower vases, the big coffee maker, glasses, napkins. But invariably I forget to resurrect our two ashtrays.

We don't smoke, so we don't need ashtrays around every day. I am not crazy about smoking, but it doesn't bother me if someone smokes at our house. So if I remember, I put ashtrays out.

If I don't remember it usually doesn't matter because not many people smoke anymore. If they do, they either politely and discreetly ask for an ashtray or they go outdoors to have a cigarette with a fellow smoker.

Smokers in America have sunk really low in the pecking order of socially acceptable souls.

I have been at dinner parties where a table full of non-smokers gave looks to a lone smoker attempting to light up that usually are reserved for terrorists.

A smoker is about as popular in a crowded restaurant, bus, store or office as a carrier of the 24-hour flu.

And gifts of cigarette lighters, ashtrays, cigarette holders and cigarette cases are almost unheard of. Either the recipient doesn't smoke or if he or she does smoke, the gift is a reminder of a failure to quit.

Most smokers are trying to quit, although some are trying harder than others.

You get my drift? There is not much smoke drifting through the air in the U.S.A.

But that is not the case in Europe.

On our recent trip across the Atlantic, we learned, observed and enjoyed many things. One observation was the widespread smoking.

Smoking in Europe seems to be a way of life at all times of life. My teen-age children who accompanied us especially were intrigued by this phenomenon.

They both work in an American supermarket where smoking is not allowed anywhere on the premises. So, they were very surprised when we went through a check-out line in an Italian food shop and the checker puffed away as she totaled up our purchases.

In a restaurant they noticed the waiters smoking as they wrote up their orders. One time, Colleen stepped away from a teller booth after exchanging money into foreign currency and said incredulously, "The teller was smoking."

One afternoon as we sat at a sidewalk cafe, we watched two men take down a large and unwieldy canvas umbrella. Both smoked as they worked. It was like watching an acrobatic performance to see if they could maneuver the umbrella without setting it afire. They were successful. I suppose it's all in a day's work.

Patrick, a cartoon aficionado at home and now abroad, discovered that even the cartoon characters on European television smoke.

Colleen wondered how everyone always knew that we were American tourists. There were many hints: we took pictures everywhere; we wore jogging shoes wherever we went; we were in a distinct minority outfitted in one-piece bathing suits on the French Riviera; our awkward attempts to speak the language of the country - only to be answered in nearly perfect English - was another clue.

But probably the most obvious tip-off was that we always were seated in the non-smoking section.

August 7, 1989

* * * *

Lakeside Show Offers the Best In Family Talent

Summer would not be complete if I did not write a column about our annual trip to visit the Barrett side of the family in Fontana, Wisconsin, on Lake Geneva.

I do this so I will be able to reminisce about the summer of 1989, without confusing the events or the people present.

For the past several summers, we have had a show at the lake. This was started by Maureen, Machaela and their cousin, Megan.

They created their own version of the Miss Lake Geneva Pageant featuring talent, swimsuit, evening gown (old high school formals) and nightgown competitions. Their brothers and male cousins were escorts.

Even though she had not entered the pageant, Grandma Barrett was crowned Mrs. Lake Geneva, a title she still holds.

One year, the girls put together a rock 'n' roll act called the

Bandanas. They called themselves Aja, Champagne and Ulla.

Planning for this year's show got under way in June when Champagne (Maureen) and Ulla (Machaela) teamed up in New Jersey with Aja (Megan). They sent a letter to all their aunts and uncles, inviting them to perform.

The rules: "You must lip sync, dance and act out a song of your choice. Costumes are not required but might be a nice touch.

The Bandanas would perform the opening and closing numbers and also would judge the performances according to "originality, creativity, lip sync and coordination."

Heavy rain forced the program to be moved to a screened porch, where the crowd was warmed up with favorite songs by the Bandanas and acts by the youngest children. There were jokes, yo-yo and dog tricks, plus a shoe-tying demonstration and an assembly of Lego block airplanes.

Then it was time for the talent show.

My partner (my husband) and I were first. We performed "Diamonds Are a Girl's Best Friend."

I thought it was a perfect selection because Marilyn Monroe and I have many similarities, but many in the audience didn't realize it even though I wore a Marilyn Monroesque dress fashioned from a black-velvet skirt found in our attic.

There were several clever acts, but I was confident that we gave a prize-winning performance - even though I forgot to lip sync at the beginning of my number. I was too busy concentrating on my wiggling.

The sentimental favorite was performed by my sister, Sheila. She sang, "We are family; I have all my sisters with me."

The number featured all her sisters and sisters-in-law as backup singers. We wore shifts Grandma had sewn for us in the '60s.

The originality prize went to Ken, his 3-month-old son, Ned, and a potty chair. They performed "Baby Love."

Ken ducked behind a table, making it appear as if Ned and the potty were doing a duet as Ken moved Ned's arms and the potty-chair lid in time to the music.

First prize went to my partner and me, but we had to share the honor with my sister, Bonnie, and her family, who did a California Raisin routine. They dressed in trash bags and actually worked up a dance routine.

Our prizes were little jars of jelly and miniature bottles of sparkling grape juice, purchased at a resort gift shop by the Bandanas.

The judges told me that they would have awarded the grand prize to Ken, if he had not won the Bert Johnson Invitational, the annual family race, earlier in the day.

August 14, 1989

* * * *

Flowers, Bows and Smiles
Make Wonderful Trim for Life

The back of the bride's gown was trimmed with a big bow attached at the waist. The train of her dress flowed from the bow and draped gracefully on the floor.

I didn't notice the bow at first because I was sitting in the middle of the pew. But after communion at the wedding Mass, our places were rearranged and I sat by the aisle.

From this vantage point I could get a good look at the backs of members of the wedding party as they kneeled at the altar. I especially noticed the bride. It occurred to me that the bow was a very nice touch on an already beautiful dress.

I found my mind wandering to other thoughts about bows. There were several in evidence.

The ends of the pews were decorated with large rose-colored ribbon bows. The ushers, groomsmen and groom all wore bow ties.

Each bow contributed to the festive air of the occasion.

Later at home, I sat on my front porch swing and continued mulling this bow thing. A bow, I concluded, is a symbol of gaiety and celebration. And as if to convince myself further, I saw, as I sat there, several large nails jutting from the front of our house. The nails are hooks to which we attach green garland and red bows at Christmastime.

The greenery and bows put me into a happy frame of mind during the Christmas season.

All this thinking about bows made me wonder if there might be some written material on the tradition or history of bows.

There was nothing about bows in the encyclopedia, so I checked the dictionary, which carried several definitions for bow, including the one in which I was interested: a knot formed by doubling a ribbon or string into two or more loops.

It intrigues me that something accomplished by simply looping a ribbon can give so much pleasure. It reminded me of other simple things - a smile, a flower, the truth - that can have dramatic results.

A smile aimed in the right direction can melt the hardest heart. A baby's first smile is cause for jubilation. A smile from a spouse, a friend, your child or a parent can light up your whole outdoors if it is natural and genuine and presented to you in delight.

Flowers are smiles and bows all at once. Petunias, impatiens, geraniums, and marigolds can't get enough of themselves. If you plant six or seven small plants in the spring, by mid-summer there's a profusion of flowers all over the flower bed.

Flowers don't ask for much - just pull the weeds around them and water them a little during the dry years. In return, they offer themselves and their beauty to us completely and unselfishly with no strings attached.

Searching for the truth, believing in the truth, living by the truth, and most of all telling the truth is a simple concept, yet it eludes us so often. But when we find the truth and abide by its wisdom there is cause for joy and contentment.

So, if your life has smiles, flowers and the truth, and if there's a bow on the back of your wedding dress, the chances are excellent for a wonderful time.

August 14, 1990

* * * *

Love of Bridge Goes to New Generation

I love the game of Bridge. But other than a monthly game my partner, Kathy Rowen, and I play with the Omaha Law League and an occasional game with my husband and our friends, the Laughlins, I play only with the newspaper.

I look forward to the bridge column featured in The World-Herald. If my husband brings home newspapers from other cities, I always look to see if there is a different bridge column. I cover up the explanation and try to figure out how to play the hand as the experts do. It's fun.

But it's more fun, of course, to play with real people. That is why when I'm on my annual vacation at the lake with all my family, I try to get a game going.

When I was about 13, my mother taught me and my siblings to play bridge because she liked to play and there weren't always people around at the lake to play with.

Bridge playing has become a lake tradition. We play mostly on the front porch but also have games outdoors - on the patio, on the lake-front, even on the pier if it isn't too windy. It would be too bad if a valuable trump card was blown into the water.

Not everyone in the family is as enthusiastic about the game as I am but this summer we played a couple hands every day. My mother was always willing to play, and when my sister Barbara arrived she was usually game for a game. That meant we had to round up a fourth. Bridge is played by two pairs of partners.

We weren't particular about the fourth's playing ability. If some-one had a slight knowledge of the game, we sat them down. We ran through several partners.

Some were less excited about this opportunity than others. Mary Pat's husband, Phil, would suffer through a few hands every so often. My husband, who's a pretty good player despite his unconventional style - I always make him be someone else's partner - would play if I persuaded him. My dad would offer opinions on the play in progress. Mary Pat never wanted to play, preferring to consult from the couch while she read her book. She was called upon frequently when we started teaching a new crop of bridge players.

A few years ago, my mother and I taught my oldest two, Patrick and Colleen, to play. Patrick enjoys bridge but Colleen thinks of it as a form of torture disguised as a social grace. This summer we worked on teaching my sister-in-law, Lilly, my children Maureen, Machaela and John, and their cousins, Megan and Joe. Machaela was the most interested. We zeroed in on her. After a couple days she really had the hang of the game. We could quit begging other family members to be a fourth, because Machaela was usually will-ing to play.

Of course, sometimes she thought it would be more fun to go sail-ing or to town. One day, as we walked to the table where my sister shuffled the cards as if she was on vacation from her job as a card dealer in Atlantic City, N.J., instead of as an art teacher in Spotswood, N.J., Machaela said to me, "I do like bridge but I don't

AUGUST

think I like it as much as you, Grandma and Aunt Barbara do."

"Obviously," I thought "this girl needs to get her priorities straight!"

August 17, 1993

* * * *

Whole House Squeaky Clean
(For One Night)

Does anyone know if there is a world record for how quickly a clean house can be messed up?

If there is one, I think the Cavanaughs could put it to the test.

I'm not talking about the deliberate ransacking of a house by an intruder. I mean the messing-up that comes with everyday living.

More specifically, I am referring to what happens to a house the day after it has been cleaned from attic to basement, from front door to garage door, from back stoop to front stoop. It doesn't last.

We just had a party in our home that required a five-star cleaning job. I had everyone hopping to my commands. They weren't happy about it, but so what.

"There's cleaning to be done and no family member is exempt from helping," I thought.

First, we did the upstairs. Then, late into the night the day before the party, we cleaned the basement and storeroom.

This cleaning rampage generated a lot of dissent.

"Who's going to look in there?" Colleen asked when I assigned her the chore of tidying up the storeroom shelves.

"You never know, so get at it," I answered.

Straightening up and sweeping the garage elicited similar grumblings and got the same reply.

"Don't let anyone come over here," Patrick told me when I had him trim the bushes on the side of the house.

"If I hired you to do this job," I said, "I wouldn't have to justify why I wanted it done."

"But you didn't hire me," he replied.

"That's right, I didn't. So when you are finished trimming be sure to pick up your clippings," I said as I walked off to deliver more orders.

We also waged a full-scale assault on the rooms that people would see. Finally, everything was finished.

That night, when all the party paraphernalia was picked up, I went to bed in a clean house. It felt great.

But it was a short-lived euphoria.

As soon as we awoke the next morning, we began undoing what we had worked so diligently to do.

The first areas of desecration were the bedrooms and bathrooms. Getting out of bed, showering and dressing left in their wake the debris of slobs.

The next target was the kitchen, where the fixings for breakfast were spilled out of the refrigerator and onto the counters and tables.

From this point the mess escalated as if it were radiating from an active volcano.

The house would have been a total shambles without some of the preventative measures I took. But I had a hard time convincing my work crew to help me. The links on my chain gang had been cut when the first party guest arrived the previous evening.

My children think I have an extraordinary desire for orderliness. They think it is fun the day after a party to sit around the house and make a new mess.

I don't. I still run around trying to maintain the unmaintainable. It is even fun for a while, because the picking-up isn't hard and, presto, things look good again.

Eventually, despite my best efforts, the lived-in look prevails and I give in to it.

I figure that we do have to live here and, besides, before long something else will come up and we will have another cleaning marathon.

August 21, 1989

* * * *

Whatever Happened to
a Spoonful of Sugar . . .?

My littlest guy was sick. He was running a fever and said his throat hurt. I made him comfortable on the couch, gave him lots to drink, wiped him off with cool cloths and treated him with children's non-aspirin tablets.

According to the package instructions he had to take four pills for his weight. Each pill was hermetically sealed in plastic and foil. The package referred to this casing as blister units. Perhaps that name was chosen because you get a blister from trying to open it.

I would try to break the package open with my hand. Then I would try using my teeth to rip it open, followed by trying to pierce it with the tine of a fork and none of these methods worked. I knew a scissors would work, but usually one wasn't handy. Out of desperation, I would grab a carving knife and try not to carve my fingers while opening the packaging.

I repeated this procedure every four hours.

He was not getting better, so I made a doctor's appointment. She prescribed an antibiotic that we requested in a chewable form because it is not as messy as the liquid medicine. When my children were babies, giving them liquid medicine was an adventure. I would pour the medicine on the spoon and then get into a bobbing and weaving match with the baby's moving mouth. The baby usually figured out that this medicine was not the pureed pears he enjoyed.

The result was medicine all over the outside of the baby's mouth and places other than the baby's tummy such as the ceiling and my clothes.

The chewables work for the post-baby years until the child is at pill-swallowing age. Getting a regular pill down some children's pipes is tough.

I have given demonstrations on how it is done by telling the sick one to put the pill on his or her tongue and than take a big gulp of water to send it sailing away to the dark sea in the stomach. She would try it, but usually after the tidal wave of drinking water flows through her mouth, the tablet remained fixed like a lighthouse in a storm.

When Matt first started his prescription of chewable tablets, he was willing to pop the pill in his mouth when I gave it to him and chew it. After a day he wasn't so agreeable.

I suggested putting the pill in a tablespoon of ice cream. He liked that idea, and we used it for a couple of doses, then he started thinking of other ways to disguise his pill. He wanted me to put the medicine into a grape. I complied with his wishes even though it was tricky getting the pill in without splitting the grape open.

Then he said he needed to try a new fruit so I cut up a peach and inserted the pill into a slice. I was beginning to feel like a caterer making hors d'oeuvres.

When Pete didn't like the medicine prescribed for his infected foot, every time he took it was an ordeal. First I had to make him a sandwich because he couldn't take the medicine on an empty stomach. He ate it while he was soaking his foot for a half-hour in a pan of water (this was part of the treatment). To keep him in one place while his foot soaked I would sometimes read to him, but most of the time I would have him watch an episode of "Who's the Boss" on television.

When it was finally time for him to take the pill, I would line up on the counter all the things he said he needed to take right afterward to kill the taste of the pill. First he had to have a glass of water, then a bite of a cracker or a cookie, then some juice, more water and cracker.

Kids. What would I do with my time without them? But I am grateful that I can keep them healthy.

August 25,1992

* * * *

Family Finally Hits Bottom Of Diaper Pile

A chapter of my life has ended - I think. My little Chewy (a.k.a. Matthew) is potty trained, which means no more diapers.

We're not even saving the diapers for another baby, which we did every other time one of ours graduated to big boy's pants or big girl's panties.

I've been diapering nonstop since 1972. Most of you will agree that's a long time. It's nice not to have to worry about diapers. But it's weird, too. I didn't realize how much easier life could be without a diapered one.

Last week, the diaper service made its final pickup. It was hard to let the diapers go. I have a lot of history with American Diaper Service. We gave birth together.

When my first baby, Patrick, was born, Mark Goldstrom gave birth to his diapering business. He delivered the diapers, and we used to chat about babies and his business.

My mother gave me a gift of a diaper service for my first couple of months of motherhood. After that I was on my own. I received two dozen cloth diapers at my baby shower, so I decided to do my own diapers. I sort of enjoyed it. It was a challenge to see how clean I could get the diapers by using bleach and then rewashing them with baby soap.

Mostly I enjoyed folding the diapers. I would flap the diaper in the air and then fold it in threes and make a pile. It was much easier than matching socks.

I would fold diapers while I watched television. We had just purchased our first color television to watch the Nebraska-Oklahoma football game, so the TV was a real novelty.

Before long, I had another baby, Colleen, to diaper. I used the diaper service until I decided to be more frugal. I went back to my baby-shower diapers.

Next came Maureen and, once again, the diaper service. Goldstrom no longer made the deliveries because as my family expanded, so did his business.

When we moved to Washington, D.C., I took along my baby-shower diapers and laundered them myself until Machaela's arrival, when we tried out another diaper service.

Before long, we were back in Omaha and John's birth was imminent. American Diaper Service has made deliveries to our front door every week since October 1980.

I finally gave up doing my own diapers. I was persuaded by the increasing laundry generated by my increasing family - and my need for dust cloths, which the diapers became.

With the diaper service, I never ran out of clean diapers. Sometimes when I was laundering my own diapers and I was caught without a clean replacement, I had to pin a dish towel over my baby's bottom.

I've used cloth diapers because disposable diapers create so much garbage. Waste management is predicted to be one of the major problems of the '90s. I have used disposable diapers, but only on vacation.

The tape tabs which eliminate the need for pins were a great invention. Diaper pins always were a problem at our house.

Once, the Dad of our family, disgusted after making several diaper changes using half-inch pins, bought 10 sets of diaper pins. For awhile we were set. But the pins gradually disappeared and we were back to using the pins from the dry cleaning.

Rubber pants also were a problem. I bought them at the grocery store and dried them in the dryer. Eventually they would fall apart. Sometimes the baby would crawl around for days with his diapers drooping out the split seams in his rubber pants.

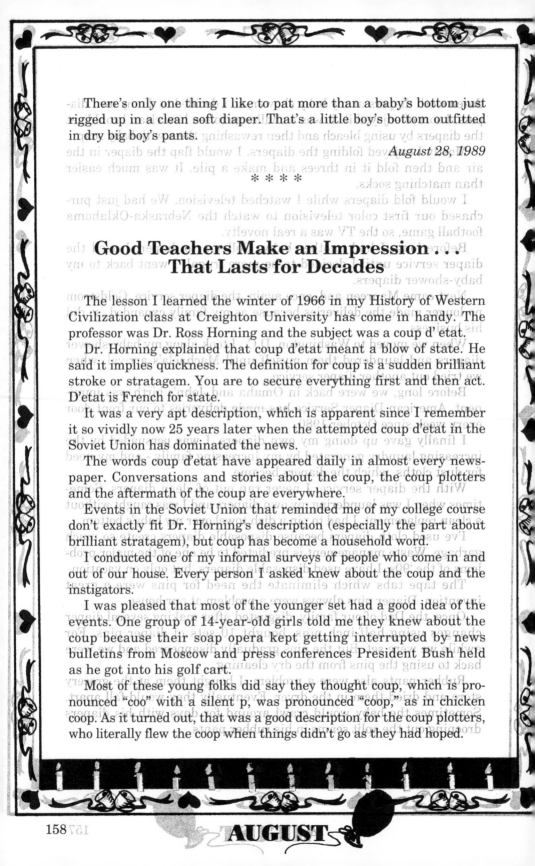

There's only one thing I like to pat more than a baby's bottom just rigged up in a clean soft diaper. That's a little boy's bottom outfitted in dry big boy's pants.

August 28, 1989

* * * *

Good Teachers Make an Impression . . . That Lasts for Decades

The lesson I learned the winter of 1966 in my History of Western Civilization class at Creighton University has come in handy. The professor was Dr. Ross Horning and the subject was a coup d' etat.

Dr. Horning explained that coup d'etat meant a blow of state. He said it implies quickness. The definition for coup is a sudden brilliant stroke or stratagem. You are to secure everything first and then act. D'etat is French for state.

It was a very apt description, which is apparent since I remember it so vividly now 25 years later when the attempted coup d'etat in the Soviet Union has dominated the news.

The words coup d'etat have appeared daily in almost every newspaper. Conversations and stories about the coup, the coup plotters and the aftermath of the coup are everywhere.

Events in the Soviet Union that reminded me of my college course don't exactly fit Dr. Horning's description (especially the part about brilliant stratagem), but coup has become a household word.

I conducted one of my informal surveys of people who come in and out of our house. Every person I asked knew about the coup and the instigators.

I was pleased that most of the younger set had a good idea of the events. One group of 14-year-old girls told me they knew about the coup because their soap opera kept getting interrupted by news bulletins from Moscow and press conferences President Bush held as he got into his golf cart.

Most of these young folks did say they thought coup, which is pronounced "coo" with a silent p, was pronounced "coop," as in chicken coop. As it turned out, that was a good description for the coup plotters, who literally flew the coop when things didn't go as they had hoped.

The benefit to be gained by following the world news is an immediate education. A year ago most grammar school students had not heard of the Persian Gulf. But six months later at the height of the conflict it would have been difficult to find an American student who couldn't pick out the Persian Gulf on a world map, plus show the locations of Saudi Arabia, Kuwait, Iraq and Israel.

To see if my hunch was true I called Dr. Horning at Creighton University. I told him my memory of his coup d' etat description. We chatted on and on about all the world events. To my delight Dr. Horning was as charming and enthusiastic as he was in 1966 in my history class. After I hung up the phone I felt I had taken a current events trip around the world.

I told him I thought children were more informed as a result of all the events in recent years. He agreed. During the Persian Gulf war children were fascinated by the Scud Missile, the Patriot Missile, the burning oil spills and the Humvee vehicles.

Dr. Horning said he learned when he spoke at grade schools that they also were aware of Islam and the different cultures in Saudi Arabia. They saw that the cities they had read about in Bible stories such as Jerusalem and Baghdad are in the same place centuries later and still are the sites of conflict.

The world is changing rapidly. Dr. Horning says our children will benefit from the constant and immediate exposure to these changes made possible by advanced communications.

And good teachers who encourage discussion, thinking and further reading about the information children acquire by osmosis from the news media will provide the real education.

That part of learning hasn't changed since 1966.

August 27, 1991

* * * *

An Open Door Is an Open Invitation
to Hordes of Flies

You know what annoys me?

I can tolerate loud radios, kids running through the house and a phone cord stretched across my path by a teen-ager draped on a couch. But add all these together and toss in a bucketful of flies and I lose my cool.

Those little bugs get to me. If they would just mind their own business or, better yet, stay out of my house, I'd appreciate it.

But that's not the nature of flies. They like to be where the action is. And they usually cause the action - whenever a fly is around, there are sure to be arms waving attempting to shoo it away.

Lately, it seems that we have had more flies in our house than could possibly be anywhere else. They come in any chance they get. If we prop open the door to carry in groceries, we bring in at least five flies per bag.

If someone opens the door to go out, there always are at least three flies hanging on the door jam waiting to fly into the house.

On a busy day, I'm sure the fly count in our house increases more rapidly than the world population.

Once you get flies in your house, the only thing to do is to try and get rid of them. There may be people who keep them as pets, but I'm not so inclined.

The logical solution would be to have the insects exit the same way they entered. For example, if a bunch of flies came in through open doors and windows, why shouldn't I have the same luck in getting rid of them?

It would seem that if the flies cruised in the front door, buzzed around the kitchen, zoomed up the stairs and zigzagged in and out of the bedrooms, they would say, "This is it? Life has to be better on the outside."

Then, at the first opportunity presented to them - a screenless open window, for example - they'd be out of here. Unfortunately, it doesn't work that way. Flies seem to approach an open door or window only to signal their colleagues, "Come on in. The air is a buzz here."

This means we have to get rid of them in other ways. The most effective way is to use Raid (you have to say that in a real loud voice). Aerosol sprays are bad for our environment and they don't do much for the upholstered furniture, either, so we usually rely on the old fly swatter method.

The other evening, even though the weather was pleasant, we ate dinner in the house instead of on the deck because the bees were such a nuisance. As it turned out, the flies who joined us for dinner outnumbered our family 10 to one.

After we finished eating, I announced a fly-swatting contest. I got

AUGUST

out fly swatters and told everyone to start swatting. I didn't partici-
pate because I want to be remembered as, "so gentle she would never
kill a fly" so I just issued the flies' death sentence.

The worst fly scenario is when a fly gets in your bedroom while
you are trying to sleep. Flies buzz around and buzz around, causing
you to dream that you hired a crop duster loaded with DDT to fly
through the bedroom to zap that fly and stop that buzzing.

When I'm getting ready for bed and hear a buzzing sound I'm
usually too tired to pursue the fly around the room with a rolled-up
magazine or a bedroom slipper. Instead, I try to chase the fly into
the bathroom and close the door. This remedy works unless some-
one opens the bathroom door and lets the fly out.

The ultimate solution is to sleep outdoors on a lawn chair. It's
doubtful that any flies would be out there to bother me.

August 28. 1990

SEPTEMBER

September seeks shoes and school supplies in the stores. Soccer games set the schedule. Sandwiches are swathed in Saran Wrap and sink into second grade lunch pails. On the 21st the oldest son celebrates his birth. The sky spreads across open spaces as the summer sun simmers down and the splendor of blooming rose bushes seizes the spotlight at sunset.

SEPTEMBER

Sunday	Monday	Tuesday	Wednesday	Thursday	Friday	Saturday
				1	2	3
4	5 Labor Day	6 Rosh Hashanah	7	8	9	10
11	12	13	14	15 Yom Kippur	16	17
18	19	20	21 *PATRICK'S BIRTHDAY*	22	23	24
25	26	27	28	29	30	

164

SEPTEMBER

That Wait For Tomatoes Was Tough

Our tomatoes are finally ripening. I've been eagerly watching over them. The plants are laden with an over-abundance of the fruit, but it seems they have been slow to change from green to red.

One of the problems is that they aren't getting enough sun. I planted some zinnia plants in front of the tomato plants and some aster plants on the side. I thought there would be enough room for all three.

When I planted the flowers and tomatoes in May, everything in the garden looked so sparse. I wanted to have an instantly mature look so I ignored written instructions that came with the plants to space them 10 to 12 inches apart. I planted them 5 to 6 inches apart.

I thought that looked nice, and it did then, but that was 3 1/2 months of growing time ago. Those early spring plantings now have increased twenty-fold.

We have zinnias and asters galore and the tomato plants are struggling behind the pretty flowers for their piece of the sky. The weeds also are doing very well in this plot. They are capable of setting up shop anywhere and everywhere.

I love home-grown tomatoes. They have to be one of life's greatest eating pleasures. The difference between a home-grown tomato and a store-bought one is so vast it sometimes is hard to imagine they are the same food.

Our whole family enjoys them. My sister-in-law, Mary Anne, brought over a bag of tomatoes from her garden, and we plowed through them with the same gusto with which we attack a one-pound bag of M & M's.

We sliced them up and ate them like finger food, and we tossed them into a salad, but most of the time the salad was bare of tomatoes before it ever reached the dinner table because they had been snatched from their bed of lettuce.

I would replenish the plump red delicacies in the salad bowls only to have them disappear just as quickly. One of my children is so fond of tomatoes that he bites into them the same way that he eats peaches and plums.

Since our tomatoes were so slow to ripen, I had Maureen pick a bunch of them and line them up on the deck railing. I thought the access to the open sky would help.

But the first time I checked to see how they were doing, they weren't there. I asked Maureen what happened. She told me it didn't

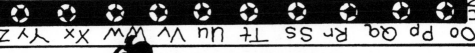

work to set them on the railing. They all rolled off because their bottoms were too round. I guess next year we'll have to grow flat-bottomed tomatoes.

In the meantime, I hope those tomatoes get a move on because I have a yen for a bacon-lettuce-tomato sandwich.

September 7, 1993

* * * *

First School Day Leaves House Empty

I am home alone. It took 20 years, but here I am, all alone (during the day) and liking it - I think.

In September of 1972, I brought home my first baby: a boy. At the time, I didn't think that I was going to go the distance and have eight children - although John and I wanted a large family.

However, my husband claims that when I was in the throes of labor, I kept mumbling incredulously, "I don't understand how anyone could do this 10 times."

I didn't have 10. Eight seemed to do it for us. Over the years, one by one, they have gone off to school. This year, my baby started kindergarten.

He's not a baby in the physical sense. He doesn't wear baby clothes or crawl on all fours. He dresses "cool" like his older brothers, keeps up with them in their roughhousing and has a vocabulary that sometimes is so grown-up it surprises me.

We don't treat him like a baby at all. I think we treat him more like he's royalty. Everything he says and does is repeated and described among our family members with such delight it is as if he has just created the words he has uttered and invented the gestures he has used.

I got the whole crew, including the older ones who hadn't departed for college yet, up moving early the first day of school. I wanted to take a family photo in front of the house. Then we all traipsed up to school to take our little guy to his classroom.

We found his desk and his name tag. The teacher told him it said Matt C. because there was another Matt who would be called Matt M. She wasn't sure if we planned to use his nickname, Chewy, at school. We decided to let Matt-Chewy think it over and let everyone know what he wanted to be called. He decided on Chewy.

Then it was time for me to leave. Neither of us cried. We were both ready, I guess.

The best part of this new milestone is that Chewy goes in the morning with his brothers and sister on the school bus. He has to get up, as Pete, a second-grader, describes it, "in the 7's" instead of "in the 8's or 9's" as he did when he was a preschooler. When the bus leaves our house I can begin my day's activities and not have to care for children until the school day is done.

It's a weird feeling. For years I've been working at home and caring for children at the same time. Since school started I have been planning all the things I can accomplish with my freedom. I'm hoping first to complete some of the summer projects I never got around to doing.

I can make plans without having to arrange for a baby sitter. I can shop without worrying about Chewy getting impatient while I browse. However, I will miss his fashion advice and his company. Once he wanted me to hurry up because I promised a stop at McDonald's after I picked out a new purse.

He asked what sort of purse I was looking for and then picked out exactly what I wanted - plus it was on sale.

This marks the end of an era for me but I am happy about having all my children in school. And I'm happiest at the end of the school day when they are home again.

September 8, 1992

* * * *

Cowboy's Goodness Spreads Far, Wide

"Joe has been in a terrible accident," my mother-in-law said on the telephone. "He's being flown from Neligh to Clarkson Hospital by helicopter."

She told me that Joe had been run over by a tractor.

I gasped in horror.

The victim, Joe Weibel, was an 84-year-old rancher from the Ewing, Nebraska, area. He has been a Cavanaugh family friend for more than 30 years.

My husband, John, and his brothers and sisters spent several weeks each summer as teen-agers working at Joe's farm.

When the helicopter arrived at Clarkson, Joe was holding his own. Since that July 19 accident, we have been amazed by his slow but steady recovery.

He remains hospitalized, but he now is at Antelope Memorial Hospital in Neligh, Nebraska.

Joe is an amazing person - a cheerleader for everyone.

The day of the accident, my brother-in-law, Tom Cavanaugh, was allowed to visit Joe before surgery.

Tom bent over Joe's bed and said, "Hang in there, cowboy."

When Joe realized it was Tom speaking, Joe perked up and said to the nurses, "Ladies, I want you to meet your county clerk." (My brother-in-law is Douglas County clerk).

Joe has the ability to make each person he meets feel special and important. I tell him that he's my P.R. man in the Sandhills. He clips my columns for others to read, and he lends my books. In fact, I understand he has been distributing them in the hospital.

The Cavanaugh-Weibel relationship began when my husband was about 11 years old, thanks to the Reverend Francis Kubart.

Father Kubart had been transferred from St. Mary Catholic Church in Omaha to St. John Church in Clearwater, Nebraska. He made arrangements for John to spend time at the Weibel farm, where Joe was living with his widowed mother.

"Grandma Weibel" was a German immigrant who told fascinating stories about the frontier days on the Plains.

Since John's visit, Joe has invited countless young people to experience rural Nebraska life. The Cavanaugh brothers remember putting up hay and working the cattle, watching part of "The Tonight Show" at the end of the day and hunting snipes.

Joe loves horses. He thinks he has 65 of them. Whenever the "redheads" (that's what he calls our family) visit, he saddles up Sundance and Ginger for the little ones to ride.

Joe seems to have an unlimited supply of cowboy boots and hats, in various sizes, for visiting city folks.

Margaret Mary Cavanaugh-Boyer learned to ride at Joe's ranch. She grew to love the country so much that she became a family practitioner with her husband, Steve Boyer, in Gordon, Nebraska.

Joe's heart is as big as the outdoors he loves, and the names in his guest books confirm it. There is a steady stream of visitors to his ranch.

His jokes are told and retold, and sometimes the jokes are translated into foreign languages because he has had international visitors.

And no one ever leaves Joe's ranch without a people-watcher - a small, beady-eyed creature made from a pebble.

The ability to give of yourself and the gifts of your life to others unselfishly and joyously is a powerful blessing.

Joe Weibel has been blessed this way, and his use of the blessing stretches as far and wide as the prairie grasses growing in his north pasture.

September 10, 1991

* * * *

Bicycle Lessons: Six Kids Down, Two to Go

The day after I gave birth to my eighth child, I was feeling rested and relaxed after 24 hours of pampering by the maternity-floor staff.

The father of the eight was not quite as perky. When he arrived for his evening visit, he practically collapsed on my hospital bed.

"You look exhausted," I said.

"I am," he said. "This afternoon when the kids and I got home from our visit with you and the baby, I gave Machaela bike-riding lessons."

"No wonder you're tired," I said.

"You know what occurred to me as I was running behind the bike?" John said as he lifted his head from where he had plopped it on the mattress.

"What?" I asked.

"That when Machaela (who is fourth oldest) learns to ride, I'll only be halfway through the bike-riding lessons. I'll still have to teach four sons."

"Maybe Patrick and Colleen can teach the little guys," I suggested.

"I enjoy doing it, but it is a workout, and I don't think it's just because I'm getting older. It was tough when I taught Patrick when he was 6," John said.

I can't speak from experience - only from observation - that giving bike-riding lessons is a lot of work. I have never taught any of our children to ride.

My job is to cheer the biker on, to assume nervous looks as the wobbly rider weaves along and to squeal every time I hear a car within a one-mile radius.

I'm good at all three assignments, especially the squealing.

John is now two steps closer to completing this fatherly task. Johnny learned to ride a while ago, and now it's Mike's turn.

When Mike first started learning, his dad ran behind him with his hand on the bicycle seat to help balance. Gradually, as Mike mastered the pedals, John would unleash his grip occasionally so Mike could solo.

When he managed to ride for 10 or 15 feet, Mike ran into the house to get me to come and watch. My jubilation was sincere. I always am amazed at how excited I get over each of my children's accomplishments.

After Mike mastered the pedaling and balancing, John let go of the bicycle seat but still ran along. Mike couldn't brake or turn, so John had to be ready to catch him when he ran out of steam or street.

Now they are working on timing and turning. Mike knows how to brake, but he doesn't know when to brake. He does so only when his dad yells the command.

This occurs when Mike is headed into a parked car, on his way over a curb or into our neighbor's flower garden.

Mike's training course is bordered by our driveway and our neighbor's driveway. Mike pedals along the sidewalk and eventually makes a turn down the neighbor's driveway, into the street and returns to our drive.

He has problems when he turns too wide and goes up the curb on the other side of the street and into a fire hydrant. That's when his dad, running beside the bike, either breaks his fall or sets the bike back on the right course.

Dad and son tell me that Mike just about has bike-riding all figured out, and when Mike learns a few safety rules, he will be able to ride solo.

Mike really is happy about this. So is his father, who is mentally counting backward - six down, two to go.

Right now, he is breathing a sigh of relief, but I believe it will be a short respite.

Pete, No. 7 child, thinks it is time for his turn.

September 11, 1989

* * * *

Professional Endeavor
Blooms From Friendship

Although the thermometer begs to differ, summer is about over, which means school is back in session. Now is the time to write the essay titled, "What I Did on My Summer Vacation."

During the summer of 1990, I wrote a children's book titled "I Can't Sleep With Those Elves Watching," which was illustrated by K.C. Kiner.

The idea to collaborate with K.C. came last May at my niece Molly Cavanaugh's high school graduation party. K.C. and her husband, Warren, and their five children are friends of Molly's parents Jim and Pat. The Kiner family usually attends Cavanaugh family gatherings.

Over the years, K.C., an illustrator and designer, and I have compared notes about our lives. We both work at home.

Our husbands take credit for the joint project of publishing a children's book. The four of us were chatting at Molly's party.

I asked K.C., "Do you have any interesting project ideas?"

"I would like to illustrate a children's book." K.C. answered.

John offered, "Kate would like to write a children's book."

This prompted Warren to suggest, "You two should do it together."

The next thing I knew, everyone was looking at me. "Why not?" I answered, "I like new adventures."

In the car on the way home my husband said, "I think you should think about doing that book with K.C. It seems like you would have fun working with her."

He was right. I have had fun and we are excited about the result. We already are working on our next book, which we hope will be the second in a series of many.

The theme of "I Can't Sleep With Those Elves Watching Me" is about being different and that it is OK to be different. The story carries a message about self-esteem, although we didn't set out to write it that way.

K.C. and I talked at length about our philosophies on life and children before I wrote the story. We settled on a story line that demonstrates our values and the importance of self-assurance, love and laughter as basic ingredients in a happy life.

The plot really doesn't have anything to do with elves, although pictures of elves are sprinkled throughout the book. We chose the title

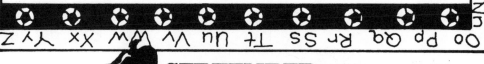

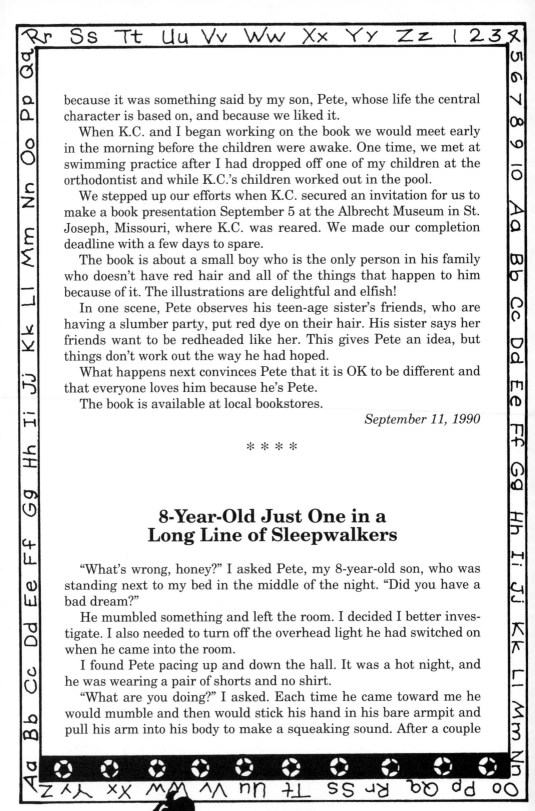

because it was something said by my son, Pete, whose life the central character is based on, and because we liked it.

When K.C. and I began working on the book we would meet early in the morning before the children were awake. One time, we met at swimming practice after I had dropped off one of my children at the orthodontist and while K.C.'s children worked out in the pool.

We stepped up our efforts when K.C. secured an invitation for us to make a book presentation September 5 at the Albrecht Museum in St. Joseph, Missouri, where K.C. was reared. We made our completion deadline with a few days to spare.

The book is about a small boy who is the only person in his family who doesn't have red hair and all of the things that happen to him because of it. The illustrations are delightful and elfish!

In one scene, Pete observes his teen-age sister's friends, who are having a slumber party, put red dye on their hair. His sister says her friends want to be redheaded like her. This gives Pete an idea, but things don't work out the way he had hoped.

What happens next convinces Pete that it is OK to be different and that everyone loves him because he's Pete.

The book is available at local bookstores.

September 11, 1990

* * * *

8-Year-Old Just One in a
Long Line of Sleepwalkers

"What's wrong, honey?" I asked Pete, my 8-year-old son, who was standing next to my bed in the middle of the night. "Did you have a bad dream?"

He mumbled something and left the room. I decided I better investigate. I also needed to turn off the overhead light he had switched on when he came into the room.

I found Pete pacing up and down the hall. It was a hot night, and he was wearing a pair of shorts and no shirt.

"What are you doing?" I asked. Each time he came toward me he would mumble and then would stick his hand in his bare armpit and pull his arm into his body to make a squeaking sound. After a couple more passes, he said, "I have to go downstairs to get a box of Kleenex." I thought that was interesting since we seldom have boxes of tissues in the house and he didn't have a runny nose.

I was able to coax him back into his bedroom where I suggested that he use the bathroom. My children claim that is my solution to every problem, but more times than not it is a remedy to some otherwise undefinable ailment.

I waited for him so I could tuck him in. It was a short wait. He ran into the bathroom, closed the door, and then instantly ran back out again and came back to where I was standing and squeaked his armpit. When I told him he couldn't have used the bathroom so quickly, he responded, "Oh, yeah" and ran in and out of the bathroom again. He did this three times and each time he squeaked his armpit.

By this time, Machaela, who was in Pete's top bunk because her bedroom was being painted, complained that it was impossible to sleep. But she ceased her protests when I reminded her that we had many similar tales to tell about her sleepwalking escapades.

The next morning Pete had no recollection of his midnight maneuvers.

My children all have had their nocturnal strolls. Luckily, no one has ever left the house.

When he was about Pete's age, I stopped Patrick as he was on his way to the garage. He was sleepwalking. Several years later he tried to convince me when I intercepted him on that same route that he was once again sleepwalking. But since he was dressed and holding car keys, I was skeptical. Of course, the next morning he couldn't remember anything about it. How convenient!

Machaela woke up one morning wondering why she was wearing her school uniform. According to Maureen, her roommate, Machaela got herself all dressed for school at about 3 a.m. and then she tried to get Maureen up as well. Maureen let Machaela know she didn't appreciate the disturbance. Fortunately, for family harmony, Machaela didn't remember her sister's wrath in the morning.

We have friends whose college-aged daughter got stuck in a closet while she was sleepwalking. The parents woke up because she was making so much racket taking boxes off shelves. At first they thought she was a burglar. When they figured out that it was their daughter, they couldn't get her out of the closet because she kept a hold of the doorknob on the inside.

As long as the sleepwalker doesn't hurt himself and the sleepwalking is not caused by a health condition, it seems like a harmless diversion during a night's rest. And the episodes make great family stories for years and years.

September 14, 1993

* * * *

She Can Quiet a Crying Baby in a Whisper

The baby's cries filled the church. They resounded off the ceiling, spiraled down to every pew and filled the ears of all the kneeling worshipers as an urgent and heart-wrenching distress call.

I couldn't see the child, but I could determine by the sound of the cry that it was coming from the mouth of a tiny baby probably not much older than a month. The volume and intensity of the sound the baby was able to emit could be envied by an opera diva.

It would have been impossible to be oblivious to the crying. I could tell everyone in church was distracted. It wasn't an annoying atmosphere created when an older child gets in a bratty mood and starts making a ruckus (my children have participated in that kind of church behavior). It was more a cry of distress. I think everyone wanted to do something to comfort the baby.

In the midst of this heart-tugging concerto, I leaned over to my daughters and whispered, "That baby needs me to whisper into his ear." They smiled and nodded in agreement.

I like to think my claim to fame is that I can quiet any fretful baby by whispering in the baby's ear. I have to qualify that to mean as long as the baby is not in any extreme physical pain or has a messy diaper problem.

There is more to this calming technique than simply bending over a crib or infant seat and whispering. First the baby has to be picked up and held close with his or her head upright supported by my hand and nestled into my shoulder, I like that part, and the baby's bottom is supported by my other arm.

Babies figure out quickly that they like to be held. A lot of times picking up a baby is enough to calm him down. One of my babies was crying anxiously moments after his birth when he was placed in an bassinet and he stopped the second he was picked up again. We all wondered how he figured out when he was less than five minutes old that that was the way to get attention.

But if a baby doesn't give up crying after being picked up, then I start the shssh, shssh whispering scenario.

I very gently and slowly whisper in the baby's ear: shssh, shssh, shssh. It's best to be standing when I do this so I can sway back and forth and up and down like I'm doing deep-knee bends. Sometimes I move forward and back, bending at the waist. I do this rhythmically and continually. It can be likened to a gentle aerobic workout but it works every time. Babies really like it.

My children have learned to use the whispering campaign. They are pretty successful with it too and have used it when they have baby-sat for little babies. A few times one of my daughters has telephoned me when she was baby-sitting because the baby wasn't quieting down. So over the phone I have guided them through the whispering routine. I've felt a little silly doing this to a telephone but most of the time it has worked.

My whispering technique works because there is no substitute for love and affection. It also can buy time when the baby is so hungry that he starts chewing on your shirt and that's all you have to offer. It works but eventually the hungry baby will realize that whispering is no substitute for the baby's formula or the mother's milk.

What happened with the crying baby in church? The mother must have a calming technique of her own because eventually the baby stopped crying and was quiet for the rest of the Mass. So I had to save my whispering for someone else's ear.

September 22, 1992

* * * *

Being Mom Long-Distance Just Isn't the Same

Today is my oldest child's birthday. Patrick is 18.

He's legally an adult. He has to sign up for the selective service, he can vote and do all sorts of other things without his parents' permission. And I'm not with him to celebrate his big day.

Patrick is away at college. He began his freshman year at Loyola University in Chicago about a month ago. He's doing just fine. I'm not. I miss him.

Patrick started kindergarten before his 5th birthday. We lived in Washington, D.C., then. The preschool teacher told me he was ready for kindergarten, so I sent him.

I never doubted that I did the right thing until 13 years later when it occurred to me if I had held him back in 1977, he'd still be at home in 1990. I know I'm being ridiculous but I can't help myself.

I spent the summer pushing away thoughts of August 23rd, the date we would take Patrick to college. But the day came despite my efforts.

When we returned home, I began unloading the car and found one of Patrick's shirts forgotten beneath our overnight bags. That's when it hit me that he was gone.

As I stood on the driveway and looked at his green-and-white-striped shirt, I felt like a part of me had broken off.

It was an awful feeling. After a bit, I scolded myself. After all, nothing bad had happened to my firstborn. He hadn't been shipped overseas as many young armed servicemen not much older than him. Only good things were happening to him.

I should be happy that he chose a good school, that we felt comfortable with his choice, that he will have many wonderful opportunities and that he was surrounded by relatives who would watch out for him and feed him on the weekends. I did feel good about all of that, but I didn't feel good about not having him at home with us.

His Dad was not feeling much better than me. Every time my waterworks began, he started feeling sad, too. We had two handkerchief sessions.

He says he has his hands full since Patrick left consoling his wife and answering questions such as, "Whose big idea was it to invent college dormitories? If they didn't have dormitories, Patrick could have been like Alex P. Keaton on the television program 'Family Ties' and lived at home until he was a bank executive."

My thinking doesn't make any sense because John and I both went away for college, and we encouraged Patrick to have that experience. I came to Omaha from the Chicago area. Now we are doing a reversal.

It's the change. Even though he'll be home for holidays and summer vacations, it won't be the same. This is what we wanted to happen. We worked hard for the past 18 years to get Patrick to the point where he would be getting an education and preparing for his adult life. We just didn't want it to happen so fast.

I've learned that there are a lot of people who feel like I do, and I never knew it. Before, if I had a conversation with someone whose child was away from home, I'd say something positive such as: "What a wonderful opportunity it is for your child to be going to that school on the other end of the earth." Now, when I talk with a parent whose child is away from home, my eyes start to fill up and we exchange a that's-wonderful-but-awful look.

It says it all.

September 25, 1990

* * * *

Parents Get a Kick Out of Sideline Cheers

The soccer ball was traveling down the field. Accompanying it was one determined pair of 10-year-old feet. In hot pursuit were several other pairs of feet, all with the sole purpose of being there when the time came to send the ball sailing through the goal posts.

At that moment, the game was being played the way the coaches had drilled. The sideline crowd was enthusiastic. One dad yelled, "Way to hustle, guys!"

It occurred to me that there are a lot of sideline comments coined for athletic events, and I think most are designed for parental usage.

"Way to hustle" can be heard at most any type of game, but there are different expressions for different sports. At Little League baseball games, you can usually hear a mom cheering "throw strikes" when her child is pitching. I imagine that is what the ball player wants to do, but it must be encouraging to have Mom there cheering.

The batter hears "be a hitter" when he or she gets up to the plate. If the bases are loaded, a hitter might also hear "ducks are on the pond."

In soccer, you hear "wake up," "boot it," "big kick now," "help her out," "be ready, goalie," "good try," "good save," "now get it out of there" and "who's guarding the goal, halfbacks?"

Some parents are more involved in the game than others. A lot of times, my sideline conversation is with another parent and it doesn't relate to any sports topic.

I look forward to the games as an opportunity to visit with friends.

Sometimes I even sit with the "enemy" when one of the parents of our opponent happens to be someone I know.

Occasionally, I'll end up next to a parent who is intent on watching the game. It can be like listening to a play-by-play on the radio, interspersed with coaching tips shouted to the players on the field. This kind of engrossed participation is not for me.

I do like to watch the game, but I'm not capable of giving the action on the field my complete attention. After a quarter of this intense watching, I excuse myself to find someone who will talk about the antics of our teen-agers and husbands.

I never yell out coaching directions, because I'm sure if I did they would be misleading. I have tried for years to figure out what you have to do to be offsides and I still don't get it. So my cheering is usually limited to clapping and yelling "yea!"

A friend says she never yells at the players either. She said she played adult soccer once and realized the game isn't as easy as it looks.

However, she says she does yell at the referee. A lot of other folks have the same pastime. Some of the comments I've heard are "Get a life, ref!" or "Wake up ref, you're missing a good game!"

At one of my son's soccer games, I took notes on the spectators' coaching comments to the players. Some of them were "show some pride," "put some hurt on the ball," "keep your foot on the ball," "stay on your feet," "dig it out," "go get 'em up the side," "it's yours, buddy," "OK, now boot it," "oh-oh, good try" and "how come they get a corner kick?"

After the game, I asked a couple of the players what they thought of all the directions. They said they only listen to the coach. The only parent's voice they hear is the one who says at the game's end, "the pop is over here."

September 24, 1991

* * * *

Skipping Town With Friends Feeds the Soul

I just returned from a girls' trip. I went with five friends to a lake house in Okoboji, Iowa. We were gone only 48 hours, but it was long enough for me to have a wonderful time and to come back renewed.

It was difficult for all of us to skip town for this adventure. We left a combined total of 26 children in the care of husbands, baby sitters and relatives. Some of those in the group had to take time off from their jobs. But mothers need this kind of break occasionally.

When my family asked me to describe what we did on the trip I told them we ate a lot, talked a lot, laughed a lot, shopped, took long walks, went boating, and then ate and talked some more.

We all fixed food to bring along and enjoyed every bit of it. En route to the lake, our larder was heavily laden with desserts, assorted sweets and snacks. On the way home, our bodies were heavily laden after consuming all those good things.

There was no lack of storytelling, philosophizing, joke-telling, analyzing, prophesying and discussing. There was so much to say and not enough time to say it.

We talked non-stop in the kitchen, in the living room, in the bedrooms, in the car, in the stores, on our walks.

We talked even when we were lying in bed with the lights off, attempting to go to sleep. We felt like the Walton family yelling from bed to bed and from room to room, carrying on and finishing up conversations and bringing up new ideas in the dark.

We had to check out the sales on all of the summer merchandise at area gift shops.

I bought a papier-mache angel for the top of our Christmas tree as a souvenir.

There was a lot of discussion in one shop about a pretty party dress that was on sale. Three of my companions tried it on. It looked wonderful on each of them.

The friend who first spotted the dress thought her daughter might wear it for a holiday dance, but she wasn't sure her daughter would like it.

The second friend liked the way the dress fit her but hesitated to make the purchase because the dress did not harmonize with her sense of fashion.

While this debate was in progress, friend No. 3 tried on the dress. She bought it.

Everyone was happy with this solution and made plans to borrow the dress.

Our hostess took us for a ride in her new speedboat, which she never had driven. We were 2 miles out on the lake when the boat experienced mechanical problems. The engine died and would not restart.

SEPTEMBER

Suddenly, the quiet late September atmosphere we were enjoying lost its appeal. There were no other boats in sight.

As our boat drifted, we read the owner's manual for guidance in an attempt to solve the engine malfunction. We couldn't find a solution. Finally, we spotted a fishing boat in the distance.

For a long time, we honked the horn and yelled "hello" in unison. I even stood on the seat and waved a white sweater, but we couldn't get the attention of the fishermen.

Just as we were nearing panic, the fishermen noticed us and came to our rescue by towing our boat to shore.

Our thanks were effusive. We gave the rescuers every reward we could imagine, including a big share of our stash of dessert bars and cookies.

While we were eating dinner at a local restaurant, one of the members of our group pointed to table of women who appeared to be 20 years older than we. It was agreed that we should try to steal away together for at least the next 20 years.

When you are lucky enough to have good friends, it's a shame to waste them. Chocolate-chip cookies are one of my favorite foods for the body, just as the company of friends is one of my favorite foods for the soul.

September 25, 1989

* * * *

OCTOBER

October opulently orchestrates an oil painting of oaks, maples and other trees onto its outdoor canvas with brush strokes of orange, yellow and red leaves. On the 6th, 14th, 17th and 21st another year is ousted as we observe our birthdays. Original outfits go outside on Halloween and odd expressions are used as an outline on the Jack-O-Lantern.

OCTOBER

Sunday	Monday	Tuesday	Wednesday	Thursday	Friday	Saturday
						1
2	3	4	5	6 JOHNNY'S BIRTHDAY	7	8
9	10 Columbus Day	11	12	13	14 MAUREEN'S BIRTHDAY	15
16	17 MY BIRTHDAY	18	19	20	21 PETE'S BIRTHDAY	22
23 / 30	24 Halloween / 31	25	26	27	28	29

OCTOBER

Columnist Bids Fond Farewell
To Boys' Friend

About three years ago, I received a phone call from Boston. The caller told me her family was moving to our neighborhood in Omaha. She had been given our name by our school principal because we had a lot of sons and she also had a young son. We talked about life in Omaha. I told her they were going to love it here. We planned to get together when they arrived.

It was right before Halloween when Joe and Sandy Kelly and their children settled in. Mike Kelly had just turned 10. He was in the same grade as Machaela and two years older than my son John. I wasn't sure if Mike Kelly (we always call him by his first and last names so we don't confuse him with Mike Cavanaugh) would want to hang out with a girl - he didn't - or younger boys - but he was willing. I invited him to our house for Halloween Hoopla and trick-or-treating.

His dad brought Mike over. He was dressed as the Grim Reaper. My boys were impressed. Pete kept calling him the Grim Leaper. All of our boys were still too young to go out trick-or-treating alone, so their dad took them. Mike Kelly went along.

When they got back to the house, I asked my husband how it went. I was afraid trick-or-treating with an escort might have seemed too babyish for a big boy like Mike Kelly. Mike may have preferred older company, but he never let on that he did.

"He seemed to enjoy himself," my husband said. "He helped out with the little guys and horsed around having fun too."

It was then I decided that Mike Kelly is my kind of kid. That's the way it has been ever since. When he comes over, he fits right into the household. The only difference between him and one of our own is he doesn't start fights.

The younger boys love it when Mike Kelly comes over. They get to do all sorts of things they can't do otherwise. I let them ride bikes up to the school playground if Mike will go with them, and they can go over to the park if Mike will watch them cross the street. He organizes football or soccer games in the front yard and makes sure the teams are even.

Over the years, Mike Kelly has made lots of friend his own age, but he still has time for "the boys."

Lately, we have had Mike as a baby-sitter. The guys suggest to their sisters that they should get baby-sitting jobs elsewhere or make plans so when I need a sitter I can ask Mike Kelly to sit.

Now it is time to say good-bye to Mike. He's moving with his family back East again. We've known about the move since the middle of the summer but we kept putting it out of our thoughts - even though every time we drove by the Kellys' house, we were reminded by the "For Sale" sign in their yard.

Then one day a "Sold" sign appeared. Mike's mom confirmed it. They would be moving the first week of October.

The Cavanaugh boys are feeling pretty low about this. John thinks Mike should stay here and be an Omahan forever.

"He could live with us."

"Yeah," Chewy agreed. "Just let his mom and dad go to that new place where they are going."

I said, "I think his mom and dad would miss him too much to let him stay here."

It's hard to imagine life without Mike Kelly around the house or without hearing his voice on the the telephone or seeing him pumping his bike up the sidewalk giving one of the boys a ride in the wagon.

But life goes on. The boys will eat, sleep, play and make up teams - but it won't be the same without Mike Kelly around to join in the action. We'll still go to the video store, but Mike Kelly won't be there to arbitrate the fights over what movie to get. There will be fort-making in the basement, but they won't look the same without Mike Kelly's ideas.

I've been trying to paint a bright picture of Mike's move.

"Now you'll have a new place to go visit." I told the boys. We got out the atlas and looked up Portland, Maine (Mike's new home) on the map.

"It's on the the Atlantic Ocean. That's cool." our Mike said.

The boys are planning on how to make money to take a trip to Maine.

"It will be just like going on a long outing with Mike's mom when she took us to the zoo or the movies," they told me. "But the best part of going to Maine will be that Mike Kelly will be there."

October 1, 1991

* * * *

Another Pile! Mother of 8 All Washed Up

When I was about 18 and had no idea of what lay ahead, I visited my Aunt Nancy, who has eight sons.

The boys ran around the room as we talked. In the midst of the confusion, my aunt got up from her chair, weaved her way across the room to a bassinet and picked up her baby.

That surprised me because I had not noticed the bassinet nor had I heard the baby cry.

My aunt must have noticed my look of surprise because she said, "This place is really wild, isn't it?"

I had to agree that it was.

"I'm going to suggest that these guys all marry young - or at least send out their laundry," she said.

At the time, I thought that was a funny remark. When I got home, I repeated the comment to my mom - also the mother of eight - and she enjoyed a laugh of camaraderie with my aunt.

Now that I am the mother of eight, I realize there was a lot of wisdom in Aunt Nancy's comment.

Laundry is a fact of life. There is no way to escape it. The only way to lessen it is to decrease the number of people who create the dirty laundry. That's why Nancy proposed early marriage for her sons.

It is incredible how quickly dirty laundry can pile up and how high the piles can become.

Laundry is overwhelming and time-consuming. I'm sure that the time I have spent sorting, soaking, bleaching and folding could have been used for more meritorious activities.

I probably could have won the Pulitzer and Nobel Prizes and collected a couple of Academy Awards, a Grammy, an Emmy and a Tony.

I have several tricks for managing the "dirty" laundry. The quickest way to cut down on it is simply to not do it.

A lot of the stuff in our dirty-clothes pile is not dirty. Clothes find their way there because my offsprings' idea of cleaning up a room is to scoop up all their clothes and put them in the hamper.

Most of these clothes weren't even worn or maybe they were worn briefly and then dropped on the floor.

I gather all of these clothes, hang them up or fold them, and put them away.

If my kids thought about it - though the possibility is extremely remote - they would assume the clothes had been freshly laundered.

Towels produce another large pile.

I'm convinced that members of my family think they will be electrocuted if they touch a towel rack to hang up a towel.

Why should they when there is a floor waiting to have things dropped on it?

These towels eventually make their way to the laundry room, where they bypass the washer and land right in the dryer. Then they are recycled back into the linen closet.

Just in case you're wondering, I do eventually wash the towels, but not when one has been used to dry someone's fingertips.

My children tell me that I could never wash clothes on television - something I have not aspired to do - because I don't sort things the way one is supposed to.

They ask me why I will wash just about everything together and then be so picky about what does or doesn't go into the dryer.

They say, "When you lay something out to drip-dry, you smooth it out and shape it up as lovingly as a mother cat cares for its newborn kittens."

I tell them, "It's exciting to me to launder something and have it look good afterward. Since laundry seems to be my calling in this world, I think I should have pride in my work."

"That's great," my children reply, "but could you use some of your pride to keep that red sweat shirt out of the load of white underwear and socks? It's embarrassing to be the only boy in gym with pink underwear."

October 2, 1989

* * * *

Backache Was Cramping Grandma's Style

The book party was in full swing. Our house was filled with people who were having a good time talking, laughing and eating.

But as one guest mentioned to me later, something wasn't right. She said she walked from room to room in search of my mother-in-law, but she couldn't find her. Finally, she came up to me.

"Where's Kathleen?" she asked. "The party doesn't seem the same without her."

I agreed. "She's in the hospital. We're hoping that she'll be able to come home real soon."

A few days later, another friend and I were chatting.

"Your party was very nice, but it sure seemed different from all your other parties without Mrs. Cavanaugh in attendance. She's always such a presence at all the things you have."

That's true. Mom C. comes to every event the Cavanaugh family has. And in an extended family the size of this one, there are lots of events!

Even if she only put her grandchildren's birthdays, baptisms, First Communions and Confirmation parties on her agenda, her social calendar would be stuffed. But that's only the tip of her occasion iceberg.

She also celebrates for graduations, political rallies, theater and art openings - plus all the holidays, especially St. Patrick's Day. This year, even Palm Sunday was elevated to major holiday status.

I'm not trying to exaggerate this - as if family obligations were a burden to endure - because to my children's Grandma, each of those days or events is a joyful occasion which she needs as a part of her life, just as a fish needs water to breathe.

Mom C. thinks of each of these events as a good time - and she hates to miss out on a good time. It's no fun being sick.

That's why her absence created such a void. We even considered postponing the party, but she wouldn't hear of it.

Her time in the hospital for back surgery was unexpected but necessary in order for her to get back to her physical well-being - and her active schedule.

It was unnerving for the family to see her suffer. We weren't used to seeing her down and out (of circulation) and she wasn't used to it, either. It was cramping her style.

And not just because she was missing out on some parties. She felt there were so many folks who depend on her.

All the Cavanaugh households received calls from friends and neighbors inquiring about her progress. Many times, the call would be from someone frail and elderly. Each time, the sentiment was the same: "Kathleen is always doing for me. Is there anything I can do for her?"

"If you have your health, you have everything."

"Your health - and the health of those that belong to you - is one of your most valued possessions."

I had always heard those sayings and I even used them when an appropriate opportunity arose. But I don't think I really appreciated the wisdom of those cliches until they applied to my life.

It's tough to see someone you love in pain - especially when there isn't anything you can do about it. You get that helpless feeling. Everything is out of kilter. Life goes on, but you get the feeling you are watching the day's events on an out-of-focus TV.

But this tale has a happy ending. The back surgery was a success. Mom C. is home. We all are thankful the ordeal is over.

Everyone is convinced she'll continue to astound the doctors with her recovery. She has tremendous motivation.

Plus, we are entering one of the family's biggest birthday seasons. I don't think Grandma has any intention of missing out on the fun.

October 2, 1990

* * * *

Family Gives Broken TV Set Poor Reception

"Mom, come fix the television. I want to watch 'Duck Tails,' " 4-year-old Pete called urgently.

After five minutes of his badgering, I stopped what I was doing and went to the TV to perform what I expected to be a simple task.

I found a fuzzy picture on the screen, something that often happens when power surges through the cable. The problem usually is easily remedied by shutting off and turning on the TV.

I tried to turn the television off but couldn't. I tried to change the station and adjust the volume but was unable to do so. Then I noticed water on the table directly beneath the control panel.

"There's water here," I said, not really suspecting foul play. I should have.

"All right, I did it," bellered Pete, who was standing behind me.

"Did what?" I asked as I wiped up the water and looked around the room for the glass from which it must have spilled.

"It was on accident, on accident," Pete said frantically.

"You spilled the water?" I asked as I continued fiddling with the controls. "That didn't seem like enough water to do any damage."

"It was a lot of water," Pete blurted out. "It was on accident."

"How did you do it?" I asked.

"With this," said Pete, holding up a squirt gun, "but it was on

OCTOBER

accident."

"Squirting the television with a squirt gun wouldn't be on accident," I answered in Pete's phraseology, "it would be on purpose - you broke the television."

"I'm sorry," Pete said again and again. Then he went outdoors to sit on the porch swing and scream out his remorse so all the neighbors could hear.

I, meanwhile, had sought out Pete's big brother, Patrick, to check out the television. Patrick confirmed my suspicions that it was not going to simply dry out and be OK.

"Why don't you take it to be repaired and take Pete along so he can learn the seriousness of this?" I suggested to Patrick.

When they returned home from the repair shop, Patrick told me that Pete fell asleep in the car (so much for profiting by the outing) but before he did he said to Patrick, "Nothing ever happened the other times I squirted at the TV."

I brought up the subject again that evening, explaining to Pete why it is important to take care of our things and that it will cost a lot of money to fix the TV.

Crying again, Pete went upstairs to see if he could find some sympathy. He did.

A couple of minutes later he appeared at the top of the stairs to tell me, "My brother, John, says people are more important than a television."

The next day, Pete's dad said, "Pete, I hear you had some problems while I was out of town."

"It was on accident," Pete wailed. "Patrick says I have to pay to get the TV fixed and it will cost a lot. Where am I going to get that kind of money?"

A good question, his father thought to himself, but a better question would be: "Where are your mom and I going to get that kind of money?"

The moral of this story is this: Pete is right; people are more important than a television. But it would be nice if the people who live in this house, important as they are, would quit breaking the stuff less important than they.

At the present rate of demolition, it will not be long until there will be nothing left around our house.

October 9, 1989

* * * *

Family Has Long-Distance Calls Down to a Science

It was about 11 a.m. when the phone rang at my parents' home in St. Charles, Illinois. When my mother picked up the receiver, my voice was on the other end.

"Hi, Mom," I said. "How are you?"

"Just great!" she responded.

"How's Dad?" I inquired.

Suddenly her voice identifier kicked in "Oh, it's you, Kathleen."

"Yes," I answered. "Did you think I was Sheila?"

"For a second, I guess I did," she answered. My mother is proud that she can differentiate the voices of her five daughters on the telephone. She says if she is temporarily stumped she fakes it until she figures out who's on the line.

My sister Sheila lives near my parents. They have a hot line between their two houses. Sheila can be in touch with our mother and father several times a day if she needs to be and vice versa. Their calls to each other aren't long-distance.

My mother was taken my surprise when I called because it was the middle of the day. "Don't you know you are supposed to wait until after 5 p.m. when the rates go down to call long distance?" she asked. In her book, daytime calling should be restricted for dire emergencies and she could tell by my chatty tone that nothing dire was imminent.

"I wanted to hear about your party and I figured I could spend a couple bucks talking to you," I said.

I try to keep my long-distance calls to a minimum, and I do try to make the calls at the cheaper times such as before 8 a.m., after 5 p.m. and on the weekends.

If I have something real quick to say and it can't wait until evening, I'll dial my parents' number right before 8 a.m. with the intention of being off the phone by 7:59 and 59 seconds. It never happens because one sentence leads to another and the clock is at 8:15 or 8:30 by the time we're done talking and the higher daytime rates have started.

My two oldest children now attend college in Chicago. I tell them their father and I like to receive letters, but they both have telephones. It's more for our benefit than theirs. We like to be able to talk to them when we get lonely.

Patrick has been away for a couple years, so I have him trained to know when it's the best time to call. We've found that the most inexpensive form of communication is to call his answering machine. A one-minute call during the day is 21 cents, which is less than a 29-cent stamp. Of course, I prefer to talk directly with him. During the lower rate periods, it only is 11 cents a minute so I can talk for three minutes and not be spending much more than the price of a postage stamp. The problem is I never talk for only three minutes.

I had to break Colleen of the collect-call habit. A one-minute call put a $2.09 charge on my bill. Her next ploy was to call us and when we picked up the phone she would say, "Call me right back." She was terrified of running up her phone bill. However, she didn't have any problem with upping our bill. What's ironic about this thinking is that I'm paying both phone bills.

My parents' phone line is a clearinghouse of information for the family. Even though I don't keep in regular direct contact with all my brothers and sisters, I know their news because every one keeps in touch with Mom and Dad, and they fill all of us in on each other.

Sometimes on the weekends I'll dial up long distance one of my siblings and settle in for a long chat. I rationalize the expenditure as being a gift of gab to myself.

October 13, 1992

* * * *

New Outfits and Haircuts
Make Picture-Perfect Kids

Tuesday is Picture Day at school.

The occasion rates high on a list of things I dislike coping with during the school year. Picture Day ranks between making a topographical relief map the day before it is due and searching, as the school bus is honking, for family memorabilia for show-and-tell on Heritage Day.

The girls think they need new outfits. Apparently, the camera will break if it photographs any garment that hasn't had its price tag clipped off in recent days.

"Surely, you have something to wear for the picture," I told the girls.

"After all, your faces - not your clothes - are being photographed."

Their response: "A nerdy outfit will make a nerdy picture."

I didn't agree with the reasoning, but I did agree to go shopping tonight.

My boys present an opposite problem. They don't understand why they have to look nice on Picture Day.

So, a compromise is in the works. I don't care if they look nice; I just want them to look decent.

John wants to wear his Batman T-shirt, and Mike thinks the soccer shirt he puts on every day after school and often keeps on all night will photograph just fine.

When I suggested that they wear pressed, button-down collar shirts and sweaters, they asked: "Is someone getting married?"

When I said no, they asked: "Then why should we wear that dumb stuff?"

We've settled on long-sleeved Rugby shirts, even though the boys think the shirts are "too fancy."

Each boy's hair was looking scraggly, so we went for haircuts.

Mike had his heart set on a buzz. I told him he was too cute and too young to have his picture taken looking like he was in Army boot camp.

Pete wanted his hair spiked. I didn't, but I let him have his way. I wanted to save my strength to argue with the other kids. Besides, Pete had his picture taken last week at preschool.

Machaela wanted a French braid, which looks pretty today but after a night's sleep will be askew and my limited hair-styling skills will be called upon in the morning to rectify it for the picture.

Deciding which photo package to buy is another dilemma. I always want to order the smallest and least expensive package available.

The day the pictures arrive, we give one of each child to Dad to put in his wallet and cut off two more pictures to send to the grandparents. That uses up three pictures per child, so why do we need 30 copies?

Every year I intend to replace last year's photo, which is in a frame with this year's photo. However, it's not last year's photo that is in the frame; it's a picture from preschool or kindergarten.

Maureen tells me we should buy the biggest package because she must exchange pictures with all of her friends.

"Isn't that the purpose of the class composite? That gives you a picture of everyone," I told her.

"That won't work," she said. "You can't write on the backs of those pictures, and my friends and I like to write on the backs of

OCTOBER

our pictures."

I gave in - as I do every year. We will order the second least expensive photo package.

I decided we may as well have something a little nicer to get stuck and lost in the back of the desk drawer.

October 16, 1989

* * * *

Fund-Raising Sales Bust the Family Budget

When you figure a monthly budget, the home mortgage and utilities usually are included, plus groceries, car expenses, medical care, clothing, tuition, insurance, credit cards . . .

I could go on but it is too depressing. However, there is one item that probably is not figured into the family budget but should be. Some months it constitutes a large chunk of discretionary income (that is if there is any discretionary income).

These sneaky checkbook deflators are known as fund-raisers.

If you were to make a random survey of 20 households, it is safe to predict that 15 would be selling something. The percentage probably would be higher if the calls were made only to families with children. They seem have the most things to sell.

Families sell things for school, church, baseball, soccer, scouts, band, drill team, debate team and lots of other activities. They offer us opportunities to purchase pizza, candy, popcorn, magazines and coupon booklets.

Sometimes we just give money- with no sequined holiday ornament or decorated cookie tin to show for it - as pledges for athletic or scholastic achievements.

Most parents grumble about these sales because they are hassles, especially for those in charge. However, success is essential to the operation of the organizations and events, so it is important to participate.

The fund-raisers also allow parents to test the outer limits of their nerves.

We are in the midst of our school's candy sale. The children take an order form around the neighborhood and to the homes of relatives and friends.

These good folks don't hesitate when they are called on to buy. They know that it is tit for tat when it comes to doorstep sales. As soon as our order form has been turned in, theirs will appear.

Of course, there are some customers who have no children, so they can't engage in reciprocal selling. Yet, they buy from our family all the time. I imagine they do this to be nice. It's unlikely that they have been saving their money in hopes that someone will come to the door selling reversible wrapping paper.

One of my big gripes is that our family has no self-control. When we sell food items, my family wants to eat it before we ever get around to selling it.

I always lay down the law that no one can have any candy unless it first is paid for. This works for the first few days.

We can always scrounge up enough change by sticking our hands between the cushions of the couch, by going through coat pockets, and by looking behind the washer and dryer. By the time this cash flow dries up, my guidelines have deteriorated from pay-as-you-eat to eat-now-pay-never.

I'm as guilty as my family of this.

Another cost effective idea would be to deliver the merchandise once the orders are filled. Instead, we never get around to it and end up paying for it ourselves.

This year, it's going to be different. I know that because there's no room in our hall closet to store undelivered candy orders.

It already is crowded with the undelivered microwave popcorn.

October 16, 1990

* * * *

Bag of M&M's Hidden in House Tests Willpower

My children say they can tell when I'm on a diet because I buy M&M's.

Unfortunately, what they say is true. The day I decide to diet I usually go to the supermarket and buy fruits, vegetables and a big bag of M&M's.

I guess my purchase is a tip-off that this is not a serious diet, but my lapse is unintentional. I always intend for the diet to be successful, even with M&M's on the menu.

I buy them because they are small. I figure, "How can a few little candies deter the scales from tipping in my favor?" But they do.

As most M&M lovers know, one "M" leads to a handful, which becomes a mouthful, which eventually forms a road of "M's" several inches wide somewhere in the hip area.

As you've probably guessed, these diets don't last long. Most days the diet is over before noon. Sometimes it lasts all day, and I eat only a few M&M's.

By the next morning, I am feeling really skinny and very deprived. So I fall off the low-cal wagon.

I don't like to weigh myself because I don't like bad news. I never weigh myself if anyone is present. I wouldn't be there either if I didn't have to be.

One of the few times I've weighed myself publicly was last summer on our European trip. There were scales in the parks so my husband, two children and I put in coins and got our weights.

Our son, Patrick, wanted to see how much we all weighed together. The only reason I agreed was because the total was in kilograms, not pounds, and I had no idea how much I actually weighed. I assumed no one else did, either.

But I was wrong. Patrick and my husband, John - who never has understood that the complete sharing of oneself taken as a marriage vow does not include information given by the bathroom scales - knew the conversion formula.

They quickly tallied the total of my bulk using the pocket calculator we were carrying to determine the rate of foreign currency in dollars.

The only other time I erred in public was at the driver's license bureau as I renewed my license.

The place was jammed. I was standing amid a crowd when the clerk summoned me loudly and with authority. "Kathleen Cavanaugh, how much do you weigh?"

I was so startled by this bold request that I forgot to lie.

The reason I even mention my diet is that I have been on it for more than two weeks. I am amazed that I have had this much willpower.

I have exempted myself from the diet on Sunday - just as we do during Lent - and on my birthday. But otherwise I have been good.

I even passed the ultimate test of having M&M's - both plain and peanut - in the house. And I haven't eaten any.

Daughter Maureen bet me that I couldn't get through the day while she was at school without having some, and I bet her that I could.

She hid the M&M's, saying that she was saving me from myself. I knew were she hid them, but I didn't get them because I would have been embarrassed had she found out.

Since I have been on this diet, I have been weighing myself. I didn't do it immediately, because I was afraid the news might be depressing. I dieted for a day and then got on the scale.

Now I am weighing myself all of the time - just in case getting on and off will speed up the reduction process.

Daughter Colleen tells me, "You don't need to lose weight. You would look a whole lot better if you would do 100 situps every day."

I did 10 situps two days in a row. Now that this diet is getting old, I am beginning to think Colleen is half right.

I don't need to lose weight; as for the situps, why do them when I can wear control-top pantyhose?

October 23, 1989

* * * *

If Kids Don't Change Their Minds!

This, too, shall pass, although right now, it doesn't seem like it will. I'm talking about Halloween.

I have a love-hate relationship with Hallowed Eve. I love the decorations, the festivities, the whimsical side it brings out in everyone and of course, the candy, but I hate figuring out the costumes.

Another mother told me she thinks there's more stress involved in the preparations for Halloween than for Christmas.

I agree. I think it's because the element of surprise is important at Christmas, which means really stressful preparations - such as shopping and toy assembly - can be handled without the children's involvement. At Halloween, children's ideas are continually expressed.

At our house, we're ready for trick or treating unless someone changes his mind. I told them they couldn't, but I'm not ruling out a last minute costume switch.

It's tempting to wait to choose their costumes because they do change their minds, but I don't recommend it - you'll end up paying for your procrastination.

You'll pay in anxiety as you rummage around the basement or attic looking for something suitable the night before the school party.

You'll pay in big bucks when you go to the store and all that's left is a $35.00 Freddie Kruger mask.

And you'll pay in guilt because your child has his heart set on being Batman or Michaelango or Bart Simpson and everything you find is passe.

This happened to me in 1977. Patrick was in kindergarten. He wanted to be Spiderman. Every time we saw that costume during the month before Halloween he'd try to persuade me to buy it - but I wouldn't. I said, "It's too soon, wait until Halloween is closer."

So he did. And when we arrived at the store, all the Spiderman costumes were sold.

I learned that Halloween is real important to children, and their costume choices have to be taken seriously.

My children plan all year long what they'll be for Halloween. I don't think March has ever passed without at least one discussion on what they'll be for October 31st.

Mike had been telling me he wanted to be Gizmo. I suggested lots of ideas to make the costume from stuff around the house, but nothing appealed to him. I resigned myself to a trip to the fabric store and a session with the sewing machine.

In the meantime, we made a trip to the store to get everyone's costume accessories. Mike spied a mask. I pooh-poohed buying it, citing the cost.

I pushed our cart a few steps past the display and stopped. I did some fast addition of the possible cost of material, a pattern, notions and time to sew the Gizmo costume. Then I compared the total to the cost of the mask. The mask's price-tag looked very reasonable. We bought it.

Now I'm keeping my fingers crossed that this idea will be his last.

Remember, parents, that each year that we successfully guide our children through October 31 makes us all one step closer to qualifying for the festivities on November 1, known as All Saints Day.

October 30, 1990

NOVEMBER

November notices night time arriving near the evening news. New beginnings are negotiated on election day. Neck warmers and knitted night-gowns are necessary as natures bares itself of all its noble nuances. Chrysanthemums nod no-way to the numbing nocturne chill. We need their blooms to be nosegays at the Thanksgiving feast.

NOVEMBER

Sunday	Monday	Tuesday	Wednesday	Thursday	Friday	Saturday
		1	2	3	4	5
6	7	8 Election Day	9	10	11 Veteran's Day	12
13	14	15	16	17	18	19
20	21	22	23	24 Thanksgiving	25	26
27 Advent Begins	28 Hanukkah Begins	29	30			

NOVEMBER

Family Is Armed to the Teeth With Multitude of Toothbrushes

There were 46 toothbrushes in the powder room vanity. I counted them after I finished cleaning out the cabinet.

This is amazing. If I were to tell my boys to go brush their teeth, each one of them would say they couldn't because they couldn't find their toothbrushes. They never can find their toothbrushes.

My logical retort should be: "If none of you can find your toothbrush among these 46 brushes, then whose toothbrushes are these?"

But instead I'd probably say, "Check the yellow bathroom because there are 25 toothbrushes there (I just counted them)," They would respond, "But none of those toothbrushes belong to me, either."

This is a mystery. We have enough toothbrushes (I counted handfuls in four more places in our house) to brush out potential tooth decay in all of the city's trick-or-treaters, yet no one who lives here thinks he owns one.

Teeth brushing has always been a big deal with me. When I was in college as a joke my friends gave me a oversized toothbrush because I wouldn't go anywhere unless I brushed first. That obsession did brush off on my daughters but my sons did not inherit it.

The toothbrushes aren't duplicating themselves underneath the bathroom sink. I am purchasing them. Whenever I see a sale price on toothbrushes, I buy several. I'll spend several minutes choosing different colors for individual family members. If the guys are along, I let them chose their own color and style.

Also, our dentist, Dr. Tim Tvrdik, gives everyone a new toothbrush when we have our teeth cleaned. These brushes are decorated with cartoon characters. Each of my guys picks out a different character.

Included in the toothbrush stash of 46 lined up in front of me now is a purple Gleamin' Glinda, a pink Sylvester, a yellow Daffy Duck, an orange Bugs Bunny, a green Road Runner, a yellow Winnie the Pooh, a light blue Mickey Mouse, a white Garfield and a dark blue Charlie Brown.

Sometimes to differentiate between the toothbrushes, I will use nail polish to paint the boys' names on the handle. This works if I remember to do it right away before the toothbrushes get lost in the vortex under the bathroom sink.

The boys must get toothbrush amnesia. A day or two after getting a new toothbrush, they forget all about it or can't find it. I suppose they might claim ownership of one or two of these 46 toothbrushes, but they would never use them. What if someone else had used it?

If I suggest finding their toothbrush from one of the toothbrushes stored under the sink or in one of the vanity drawers, my idea is rejected in a big hurry. You would think I was suggesting that they stick the toilet plunger in their mouths among their pearly whites (although their teeth at this point are not pearly white but cruddy yellow) instead of a toothbrush whose life's work has consisted of being lathered up once with toothpaste to make a couple of perfunctory swipes over someone's 6-year molars.

I try to convince them that I have matched each toothbrush with its rightful owner's set of incisors. But to put their minds at ease, I suggest sterilizing the toothbrush by holding it under the hot-water faucet.

Occasionally, they will go for that idea if I make a ceremony out of it. Once I tried an en masse sterilization of toothbrushes by boiling them in a pan of water. It didn't work. All the bristles melted.

Maybe a wise solution would be to feed the boys Milk Bone dog biscuits - touted to clean a dog's teeth - and forget the toothbrushes.

November 3, 1992

* * * *

Clicking TV Remote Gets Out of Control

Let me explain clicking to those of you who are not clickers or who aren't married to a man who is (studies - at least the ones I've conducted - prove that it is a mostly male thing).

Clicking is the sport of constantly flipping through the television stations with the use of a remote control device.

The male species, prone on a couch or in a reclining chair situated in front of a television, customarily engages in this activity. He holds the clicker (TV remote control) in one hand and the newspaper in the other. His refreshments are within arm's length.

With this arrangement he can snack, read and switch among 40-plus stations all at the same time. He must be in a reclining position, because it is exhausting work to keep all those story lines, news stories and sports scores straight.

NOVEMBER

If he should happen to nod off during this exercise (I know I'm using the word exercise loosely), the easiest way to rouse him is to try to pry his fingers off the clicker so you can change the channel to the "Home Show." He'll pop right up and start clicking away again.

When I'm sitting with my husband attempting to watch TV, it seems as if I just get interested in something when he clicks to another station.

Sometimes when I'm watching with him I get confused. We'll be watching a sitcom and the newspaper I'm reading momentarily diverts my attention. The next time I look up, the station is on a murder mystery, except I didn't realize that it had been changed. Then I wonder what I missed in the plot to make the tempo change so dramatically.

It used to be that if I wanted to watch something, I'd turn on the television, find the station the program was on and sit down. If I wanted to change the station I'd get up and change it at the controls on the television set.

Now I've become a clicker. I'm really surprised at myself. I never thought I would succumb to such a short attention span attraction as clicking through stations.

The recent election changed the way I watch television. I became a news junkie, especially during the school day when I would be home alone with no one but the pets (they never got into the campaigns).

One day I picked up the remote control and figured out how to operate it. I had to see what all the newscasters had to say and what the different polls predicted. First I'd scan ABC, NBC, and CBS for updates and then to get my fill of the day's events I'd flip to CNN, C-SPAN, MTV and the Weather Channel (to see what effect the weather would have on the voter turnout).

As I flipped through the stations sometimes I'd pause at "E," the entertainment station or catch part of an old Mary Tyler Moore show on Nickelodeon.

I quickly learned the station channel numbers for cable television and learned how to glide from one station to another with the timing of a more experienced clicker. I learned to gauge how much time I had to survey the other news stations to make sure I didn't miss any part of a news story on another station.

I've discovered using the clicker is fun. But I also realized that our TV room is only big enough for one clicker, that too many clickers can ruin the shows, and whoever holds the clicker rules the TV set.

NOVEMBER

I used to think the clicker was an annoyance, and I was relieved when it would get lost down behind the seat cushions and no one would search for it. I still think it is an annoyance except when it's my turn to use it. Then it's a great invention.

November 10, 1992

* * * *

Here's to Life and Marriage

My brother, Billy, was married last weekend. The ceremony was long awaited.

Billy is the baby in a family of eight brothers and sisters. He is everyone's favorite, which means we all were choosy about choosing his wife.

When Lilly came onto the scene, we felt Billy was headed in the right direction. We liked the sound of their names together - Billy and Lilly - and besides, Lilly was a good sport.

She put up with and even seemed to enjoy the commotion when everyone got together at the lake, and she was willing to wash dishes, a most important factor in fitting into the family.

Last spring, when Billy and Lilly called around with the news of their engagement, there was a chorus of "it's about time" and "that's great."

The wedding date and location - our hometown of St. Charles, Illinois - were set. And the fun began.

Our summer visit to the lake was spent reading bridal magazines. My daughters and their cousin loved helping Lilly decide among the hundreds of bridal gowns shown in the magazines, and the girls also enjoyed visualizing themselves in one of the beautiful dresses.

As the wedding day approached, everyone helped with the preparations. For example, my sister, Sheila, prepared lasagna to feed the masses arriving for the weekend. And I provided the masses to eat the lasagna.

But we didn't just eat. On the agenda posted on the refrigerator was a leaf-raking contest at the future bridegroom's home. My masses were entrants in that contest.

The day before the wedding, I checked my gang and some of the cousins into a motel. I felt it would be easier if we cleared out of the house before it was time for everyone to dress for the wedding.

We had three motel rooms with three bathrooms and no hot water in any of them. I couldn't imagine how I would shampoo 12 heads in cold water, so I went out and bought doughnuts. By the time we had eaten the doughnuts, the hot water had returned. Everyone was clean and gorgeous by wedding time.

Lilly was born in Yugoslavia. Her family immigrated to Chicago when she was about 6 years old. Several customs from her homeland were included in the wedding celebration. My favorites were her father's kiss on each of the bride's cheeks after he lifted her veil and gave her away, and the wonderful Croatian pastries served after the ceremony.

The reception was held at Hotel Baker along the Fox River in St. Charles. My parents had their wedding reception there in 1944. It is a grand old hotel with an oval ballroom and a lighted dance floor.

Dad told me as he led me around the dance floor that he and my mother used to go to the hotel for dinner dances. It sounded very romantic.

I have many fond memories of Hotel Baker, but Billy and Lilly's reception was the first time I had been there for a party.

When I was a little girl, a friend and I would go into the hotel lobby and pretend that we were rich ladies. If we had money, we would have a snack in the hotel coffee shop.

When I was in high school, we would stop off at the Baker after football games to comb our hair in the fancy powder room before going to dances in the basement of the municipal building.

My mother and father got their marriage send-off at Hotel Baker, and almost 46 years later they agree they have had a wonderful journey through life.

I think Billy and Lilly made a smart move by repeating family history. Life is wonderful all of the time, but all the more so when you can celebrate it with family and friends.

November 13, 1989

* * * *

NOVEMBER

Driver's Credibility Goes Down the Drain at Car Wash

"Dad, you're a better driver than Mom," said 4-year-old Matthew.

"Oh?" my husband answered, "Why do you say that?"

"Because Mom got a big dent in the Suburban and we had to take it to the fix-it place."

I interceded on my behalf. "I admit there's a big dent in the side of the truck, but that doesn't mean Daddy is a better driver than me because I wasn't actually driving when it happened."

"Did someone in another car hit you while you were parked - like Colleen did to her friend's Dad's car when it was parked in front of his house?" one of the little guys asked.

"Did the car go out driving on it's own, like in the television show, 'My Mother, the Car,' and get in an accident? Or did robbers take the car and run into something?"

"Nothing like that happened," I said.

"Well, how did it happen?" everyone wanted to know.

"It happened in the car wash," I told them.

"In a car wash? How?"

"I had an accident in the car wash."

My husband, the comedian, asked: "Did the gorilla in the Gorilla systems car wash attack you?"

"Did you wreck the car wash?" someone else wondered.

No, I don't think I hurt the car wash.

Although, we were stuck in the car wash for quite a while. I took Aunt Cathie out for a birthday breakfast, and on our way home we stopped for a tank of gas, which included a free car wash.

I pulled into the car wash, which is one of those small systems attached to the gas station. My vehicle is large, but I've been washing it there for a long time and never have had any trouble.

The problem arose when the washing apparatus stopped. Ordinarily, I would have been able to drive straight on through to get out, but the door on the other end was closed.

"This is kind of a tricky spot to maneuver out of," Cathie said as I started to negotiate my way backward. I assured her all was fine. A second later, the car wash and the car fused together.

I couldn't get out the driver's door, so Cathie crawled under the dripping rotary brushes to get help. It took two men using a lot of muscle and fancy footwork to release us. It was an embarrassing predicament.

We've had some good laughs over this. Although, I think I would have laughed a lot harder if it weren't going to cost so much to fix the dent.

Before this incident, I thought the worst thing that could happen in a car wash was to leave the car windows down and have all the water and soap shoot in and ruin the upholstery or my hairdo.

I was relieved that I didn't have to fill out an accident report. It would have been difficult to describe what happened because I'm not sure if the car wash hit me or if I hit the car wash - or if we met halfway.

Until this happened, I was able to cite an impeccable driving record - no traffic tickets or insurance claims to validate my credentials as the traffic cop of our family.

My husband must listen to a recitation of the rules of the road handbook whenever we ride together.

I point out the speed limit when I think he's going too fast. I announce the amount of the fine for exceeding the speed limit and explain how much our automobile insurance will go up if a speeding ticket is recorded with the Department of Motor Vehicles.

My driving credibility was washed away in that car wash. The drivers in my family never will put my safe-driving preachings into practice.

Although, I doubt they ever did. The only advice I can legitimately give is to always drive a clean car because you never know when you will be in a car accident.

November 13, 1990

* * * *

Project Dangles by Apron Strings

Last Spring when I was shopping with one of my daughters, she liked the sleeveless shift dresses we saw in the store. They reminded me of the styles I wore when I was her age. Back in the 1960's, my grandma made my dresses. The 1990's version of the dresses seemed expensive. I said to Colleen, "Maybe we should get a pattern and material and make dresses."

"We don't even have a sewing machine," she told me. "Yes, we do." I told her "Grandpa and Grandma Barrett gave me one for my birthday in 1970.

"How come I've never seen it?"

"Years ago I took it over to Aunt Cathie's house because she was going to try fix the sewing tension for me."

"Did she?"

"No, she was just as frustrated with it as I was. The sewing machine is still at her house."

"Why don't you take it to a real repair shop?" my oldest daughter suggested.

So I did, but after the sewing machine was overhauled I never got around to making the dresses for Colleen. The ones in the store were eventually marked down so we bought them. It was the apron project that got me to resurrect the sewing machine.

For my new children's book, "Pete's Lost" which will be out this month, K.C. Kiner, the illustrator, said that since we had Christmas sleep shirts designed for our "I Can't Sleep With Those Elves Watching Me" book it would be fun to have an apron for our new book.

"I could make a silk screen design using the scene from `Pete's Lost' where the mom and the little boy, Pete, are dancing in the kitchen." K.C. suggested.

We decided to call the design "The Kitchen Dancers".

I found that we could have our art work silk screened on some plain muslin or solid colored aprons but I didn't think plain aprons would be special enough. I decided we should make the aprons ourselves and have the art work silk screened on separate pieces of fabric and appliqued to the apron.

Before this project I had never given much thought to the construction of aprons, but now I am totally versed in in the process. I have involved numerous others in this undertaking, too.

Each time I went into a fabric store to search for materials, I explained what I was doing to the salesclerks who probably wished they never asked, "May I help you?" By the time I finished explaining my ideas, each felt like it was her project.

Although I found someone to sew the aprons, I did make a sample design. The kids were really excited when I got out the sewing machine. Everyone wanted a turn to work the foot pedal.

The children were amazed that I knew how to operate a sewing machine. Actually, I was surprised that I remembered how to thread the machine - it had been so long since I had done it.

My handiwork could not win a ribbon at the county fair, but I was proud of my finished apron.

However, my seamstress status was short-lived. My talents were sent to the cutting table, where I was able to use the left handed scissors I had purchased on one of my fabric-shopping missions.

Amy, my college student helper, and I cut out four dozen aprons on the kitchen table. The aprons are undergoing the next phase of assembly elsewhere.

This "Kitchen Dancers" apron project maybe a crazy idea, but the aprons are as cute as our book "Pete's Lost" and besides, life wouldn't be nearly as much fun without at least an occasional crazy idea.

November 12, 1991

* * * *

Family Has Renewed Faith
After Cancer Scare

The Webelos meeting was in progress. I had all the scouts sitting at the table. We had just completed flag-folding and we were discussing the pledge of allegiance when one of my girls brought me the phone.

My sister, Sheila, was on the line calling from her home in the Chicago area. When I heard her voice, I knew something was wrong.

"I've got bad news about Dad" she said.

"What is it?" I asked as my mind raced from one horrible thought to another.

As she started to tell me, her voice broke. "Everything could turn out fine but he just found out he has a malignant melanoma." She quickly recited all the details and what was supposed to happen next.

I told her that I was in the middle of a cub scout meeting and couldn't talk but I would call back as soon as it was over.

My insides felt like something heavy had landed on top of me and I couldn't lift it off.

I wound up the meeting in a hurry. Then the phone calls began. I called my parents, I called my sisters and brothers, they called me and they called each other. Once I had all the information and felt the best medical decision had been made for Dad, there was nothing left to do but wait for the results of a medical test and to pray for a favorable report.

Suddenly, the world looked different. I used to have the attitude that bad things only happen to other people. They would never happen to me or my family. Over all, that has been true. But as I've grown a bit older, I'm feeling less invincible.

I had to continue with all my activities. Luckily, I had plenty to keep me busy. Everyone was trying to be upbeat and positive. After all, it could turn out fine.

The children were worried about Grandpa. We made a package of new school pictures and letters to send off to the grandparents so they would know we were thinking about them.

This optimism would work for a while but every so often, a cloud of gloom would darken my bright outlook. At those moments, "what if" questions consumed me.

Everything I looked at and every where I went seemed different than it did before. I was nostalgic, sentimental, philosophical and scared. I also was glad to have a strong faith in God. It sure helps.

Late one afternoon during the waiting period, while I waited for Maureen to come out of a store, I watched the sunset. It was a very pretty one. The formation of the clouds and the colors of the sky were so spectacular, it seemed clear that we are part of something greater than ourselves and the immediate circumference of our lives.

I always felt that but it was a detached acceptance. It made me feel vulnerable and hopeful at the same time.

The report on my Dad came back clear the Saturday after the first diagnosis and his surgery was successful. The moment I received the news, I felt like the heavy load that had toppled on me was lifted off. Tears of relief and gratitude appeared.

After such an incident, nothing will be the same. To teeter on the edge of heartbreak and to be rescued is a blessing our family so gratefully and thankfully has embraced.

This Thanksgiving, I wish everyone the joy a thankful life brings.

November 20, 1990

* * * *

Show-and-Tell Appearance
Requires Give-and-Take

I waited to plan my day until I received a phone call at 8:30 a.m. I knew I had to be available when I was called upon.

The caller was my son Mike. It was show-and-tell day and I had to deliver Mike's show-and-tell to school. It was too big for Mike to transport on the school bus.

When he left for school he wasn't sure when show-and-tell would be, so he had to ask the teacher and then call to tell me the time.

Mike's show-and-tell was a pirate ship that he built with plastic Lego blocks. It is about two feet long and 18 inches high. It has lifeboats, treasure chests, pirates with muskets and cutlasses, captain's quarters, and monkeys hanging on a rope. It is very elaborate and he is proud of it.

Mike was worried that his project might be wrecked at school, but I was worried that it might be wrecked while I was transporting it to school. I planned to carry it on a large, thin piece of board. But then I spied the laundry baskets. They worked perfectly.

Putting together a pirate ship takes a lot of patience - more than I have for such a project. But I did have the patience to help Mike decide what to take for show-and-tell.

Mike first asked if he could take the dog for show-and-tell. I nixed that idea because I took her last year for Pete's show-and-tell.

"How about the turtle?" Mike asked.

"Didn't we do that already this year?" I asked.

"Oh, yeah," he said. "I forgot."

I wasn't surprised that he rejected my suggestions. Pete had done the same thing earlier in the week. Pete wanted to take the cat for show-and-tell. Luckily, I had an excuse so I couldn't do it that day. I proceeded to walk around the house suggesting alternative ideas. He finally decided to take a carved Russian toy.

Joe, the son of my neighbor, Chris Sodoro, had to take something for show-and-tell that required the use of the five senses. Joe decided before bed to take the Santa hat because you could feel and see it. His mom was happy to have that settled so easily.

But by morning, Joe had decided the Santa hat wasn't good

enough and a frantic room-to-room search began for something that was. The kindergartner finally chose a holiday shaker because you could see it, feel it and hear it.

Once this was settled, Joe forgot all about it and left his show-and-tell at home. Chris said she felt compelled to take it to him at school. The last time Joe forgot his show-and-tell at home, he did a no-show-and-tell-all performance about his family.

November 24, 1992

* * * *

Son's Reading Gives Message: Sharing Is Love

Mike was very excited when he arrived home from school.

"I have a part in my class Mass this week." he told me.

"You do? That's great." I said. "What part?"

"The first reading, which means I walk in at the beginning of Mass with Father."

"Wow, what until Dad hears about this. He'll be really excited."

That night, Mike and his dad practiced his reading. Mike already had practiced in church so he would be familiar with standing at the podium and speaking into a microphone. Mike said that it was kind of scary reading in front of people, but he was excited.

The night before the school Mass, I made sure Mike had a shower and his fingernails trimmed. I ironed his uniform shirt and pants (usually I just try to get them out of the dryer before the wrinkles set in). Then I tried to persuade him to wear his uniform sweater for the reading - an idea he vetoed as if I had suggested something really out of the ordinary.

"We don't have to wear our sweaters unless it is First Friday Mass, and my Mass is on Wednesday." he told me.

I put the sweater in his book bag just in case he changed his mind and wanted to wear it.

He didn't, but when his dad and I saw him standing at the podium on the altar to begin his reading we thought he looked wonderful.

The theme for the Mass was sharing. Mrs. Atencio, Mike's teacher, and Mike's third-grade classmates at St. Joan of Arc School made a banner that carried the message that sharing is love.

At our house, we have a saying: It's not worth having if it can't be shared. We usually use it to settle disputes over toys and fruit roll-ups. But since Mike's reading at Mass, I have been thinking of other examples of sharing.

My nephew, Max, began kindergarten this year in Downers Grove, Illinois. My sister, Sheila, his mother, who also has a 2-year-old son, gave birth to a baby girl shortly after school began. "I have a neighbor who takes Max to school every day." My sister told me. "This neighbor says she's happy to be able to help me out."

When I was moving back to Omaha from Washington, D.C., I had an older friend helping me out. I was pregnant with my fifth child and quite overwhelmed with everything I had to do. My friend said to me when I expressed my gratitude, "Someday you'll be my age, then you can help out someone who is in need."

I told Sheila that maybe someone helped out her friend once and now she is sharing the goodwill she experienced by taking Max to school.

Kind acts should go on and on. I have been the recipient of kind deeds passed on. In the middle of our weekend snowstorm, I had a book-signing party. Attending was my good friend, Janice Hanna. We were next-door neighbors from 1971 to 1976. I introduced Janice to Chris Sodoro, who is my present, next-door neighbor. Right away, Janice and Chris were soul mates because they have shared the hair-raising experience of dealing with me and my family on a regular basis.

As I stood with these two friends, I felt enriched. Both woman have shared themselves with me unselfishly, unconditionally and with a genuine good heart and humor.

The message in Mike's reading was a spiritual one that instructs us to take bread for ourselves and share it with an orphan and share our clothes with a beggar so he can be warm. But it seems that this theme is also the spirit of the Thanksgiving holiday.

America is a nation created to be tolerant of differences, generous with our blessings, and always caring for others even when it is difficult to do. It will remain this way if we remember that sharing is love.

November 26, 1991

NOVEMBER

DECEMBER

December is decked with the drapings of the season and there's a daily dash of things to do. Children dream of the delights Santa Claus is destined to bring. Poinsettias are decorating Advent's doorstep when a distressed duo traveling by donkey appears. As the darkness departs on the 25th the sky dazzles because the Christ Child is delivered.

DECEMBER

Sunday	Monday	Tuesday	Wednesday	Thursday	Friday	Saturday
				1	2	3
4	5	6	7	8	9	10
11	12	13	14	15	16	17
18	19	20	21	22	23	24
25 Christmas	26	27	28	29	30	31

Barnyard Balm Soothes Hands
In an Odd Way

It's rubber-glove season again. As soon as the outdoor temperature drops, I start wearing rubber gloves to wash dishes and scour the sinks.

From April through November, I usually can plunge my bare hands into any sink full of dirty dishes with no difficulty. (Except at my mother-in-law's house; she uses hotter water to wash dishes than she uses to make tea.) But when the house has to be closed up for the winter, the cracks on my hands open up and I suffer.

So, I wear rubber gloves to avoid dishpan hands so sore that even Madge on the Palmolive dish-washing detergent commercials can't cure them.

Most winters, I go through a couple of pairs of rubber gloves. A gloved finger will spring a leak after a fork pierces it, or one glove will get lost in the abyss under the kitchen sink.

On occasions when I've been desperate to clean the kitchen and I haven't been able to locate a non-leaking pair of gloves, I've worn a right-handed glove on my left hand. This works fine as long as I'm washing stew kettles and not crystal stemware.

I will wear leaky gloves, if that's all I can find. I would rather have water seep through a little tear than plunge my hands into a sink full of hot water. However, it does give me the creeps to stick my hands into soggy gloves.

I don't really like wearing rubber gloves. My fingernails get cleaner without them. At least that's what I tell my kids when I want them to do the dishes.

I take a lot of physical and verbal grief over my winter hand condition. When I was young, my mother made me put glycerin on my hands and sleep wearing little, white-cotton church gloves.

When I was in high school, my Dad got involved. He was worried about my chapped feet. (I insisted on walking to school wearing flat shoes and nylon stockings.) He got some pork tallow from a butcher and had me lather my feet with the tallow before I went to bed.

The next morning, my feet were nice and soft but they smelled like pig fat - which is not the way a high school girl attracts dates.

I don't have chapped feet anymore. And I don't soothe my hands with glycerin. Instead, I lather up at night with bag balm, which is used to soften the udders of milking cows. (Another barnyard remedy; however, this one doesn't smell). I cover my hands with knee-high athletic socks and climb in bed.

I may look odd, but it doesn't matter - except on nights I have to exert authority. One night, I stormed from bed to the top of the basement stairs with the intention of lecturing a rowdy throng of teen-agers gathered below.

As I completed my "That's enough carrying on for tonight" speech and turned around, clad in my pink flannel nightgown, I heard one of the teens ask incredulously, "Does your mom have socks on her hands?"

They can make fun of me if they choose, but this treatment does work. I just have to remember when I get up in the morning to walk on my feet instead of my hands.

December 3, 1991

* * * *

Noses Wrinkle At Bean Soup

The bean soup is gone. I just finished washing the pot.

My husband, John, made the soup, and despite contradictory remarks from other family members, it was delicious.

John soaked the beans overnight in a pot of water.

The next morning, he chopped an onion so pungent that it brought tears to the eyes of everyone eating breakfast in the kitchen.

After adding other ingredients such as whole tomatoes and ham hocks, John placed the pot of soup on the stove to simmer.

This last step prompted a debate on the definition of "simmer."

I said simmer means that first you bring what you are cooking to a boil and then you reduce the heat. John thought otherwise but my opinion prevailed.

John left for the office and I was left in charge of baby-sitting his soup.

My instructions were to stir the soup occasionally until 3 p.m., at which time I was to remove the pot from the burner, let it cool and then place it in the refrigerator.

The recipe recommended refrigerating the soup overnight before reheating. We took a shortcut because we wanted to serve the soup that evening.

While running errands, I bumped into a neighbor who is an excellent cook. I told her about the soup-making effort and asked her advice: "What do you do with ham hocks?"

I shared my friend's advice with John: "You should take the ham hocks out of the soup to cool, remove the meat from the bones, and break the tomatoes into pieces."

When dinnertime arrived, we were set for a delicious meal. We had our soup, warm bread and a salad.

But there was a missing ingredient: hungry mouths. Five of our eight children were out for the evening. One of them left when he heard what was on the menu.

This left us with three little guys to share the soup, which none was eager to try, despite my exclamatory remarks.

Mike succumbed to testing it after I bribed him with a box of candy canes. The other two guys ate the bread and I ate their soup.

There was enough leftover soup to be served the next evening with a spaghetti dish I had prepared.

Here's a sampling of the commentary:

John: "This soup is savoir faire." He kissed his finger tips.

Maureen: "What's that supposed to mean?"

John: "It means it is an old family recipe handed down from the cabinets."

Machaela: "It is? I thought you got the recipe off the back of the bag of beans."

Me: "It's time to eat. Everyone come to the table. We're having Dad's bean soup."

Pete: "I already had my bean soup last night."

John: "There are several people here tonight who weren't home last night to get some soup."

Mike: "That's right. They should get the most."

Colleen: "This bean soup is good but how come you put so many beans in it?"

Me: "I'll take everyone's leftovers but you have to at least try the soup before you can have another crescent roll."

Later, as I washed the bean pot, Pete came up to me. I asked' "How did you like the soup?"

"Fine," he said, "but I didn't eat much. I didn't like the leaves in the soup."

"You mean the parsley?"

"They're gross. Can I have something good to eat now, like Teen-

Age Mutant Ninja Turtle cereal?"

Pete is our connoisseur of fine dining.

December 4, 1989

* * * *

Decking the Halls
Tests Survival Of Holiday Spirit

The outdoor Christmas decorations are up. It is not a winter wonderland out there, but it does look nice.

I wanted to hang evergreen garland to frame the front door and put lights and red ribbons on it. I've seen that done at other homes. It looks so pretty, but we couldn't figure out how to hang the garland.

The molding around the door is metal and the house is stone; therefore, it isn't easy to find a place to hammer a nail. I wasn't going to let something like a stone wall keep me from creating the look I had in mind, but it did.

My next idea was to hang the greens around the garage doors, but the garland was too short. So, I opted for the living room windows. Patrick hung it and placed a wreath in the middle. I loved how it looked but thought I needed to make the house appear more symmetrical.

"We should do the same thing over the dining room windows." I told my son, who also is my assistant.

"We should," he agreed. "Why don't you buy some more greens, and you might as well get some more lights. I can't get those others to work."

That was easy for him to suggest since we weren't spending his money. I went to the nursery and ordered the length of garland I needed for the dining room windows.

"Can you use a few more feet of greens?" the salesperson inquired. "It's more reasonable per foot to buy it by the roll."

"Sure, why not. I'll find a use for it." I replied. I also purchased wreaths, the lights and yards of wide red ribbon to make bows. I thought the pre-made bows were too expensive, and I could save a couple of dollars by making my own. Of course, that was before I tried to make them.

I did find a use for the roll of greens. It was much more than I needed for the dining room so I put it over the garage doors, which left the dining room windows looking neglected. I hung one of the wreaths over the windows. It looks OK but still needs garland around it.

I hung the new lights over the garage door. I wanted to light up the wreath, too, but I was out of lights that worked. So I sat down on the floor near an electric outlet and tested the bulbs until I found the culprit that was keeping the whole strand from lighting.

As we worked, I was bothered that there were so many leaves still in our bushes and flower gardens. I wanted to get a rake and clean them out, but Patrick tried to discourage me. I think he was afraid I would make him do it.

I got the rakes anyway and while we raked I reminded him, "We haven't put the lights in the oak tree yet."

"That's Dad's job," Patrick said. "He likes to get out here with a ladder and stick the lights way up on the branches. He always picks the coldest day to do it and he has me help him."

"Well, it's all part of getting into the Christmas spirit," I told him.

"So is roasting chestnuts on an open fire. When do we get to do that?"

"Just as soon as we finish decorating," I answered. "Now do you think we can run an extension cord out to the mailbox and set up those computerized bells that play Christmas carols?"

December 11, 1989

* * * *

A Brush With History
. . . Spirit of Christmas Spreads All Across Eastern Europe

It's Christmas, and there is hope in the world.

I experienced some of this hope last summer when my husband, John, and I took a trip to Europe to celebrate our wedding anniversary. We were married in Frankfurt, Germany, and wanted to go back to where it all began. We took along our two oldest children, Patrick and Colleen.

As we were planning the trip, each of us had different ideas about where we should go.

Patrick, for instance, wanted to go to Berlin. My husband said if we were traveling to Berlin, we might as well continue on to Czechoslovakia. He always had wanted to see Prague.

I balked at the itinerary. It seemed like too much trouble to get visas and train reservations for eastern Europe.

Today, my worries seem insignificant. I'm glad we took the trouble.

We traveled by train from Frankfurt to West Berlin, where the atmosphere was lively. Big stores were stocked with expensive merchandise; streets were jammed with luxury cars; elegant hotels, restaurants and nightclubs were everywhere; and people were fashionably dressed.

From West Berlin, we entered East Berlin and traveled by train to Prague. Our timing was propitious. We saw what life was like behind the Iron Curtain months before the curtain was lifted and a new act in the theater of life began.

It was a short subway ride from West Berlin to East Berlin, but the contrasts in cities couldn't have been greater.

After a border check, we explored the city. Few people were on the streets; stores seemed to carry little merchandise; restaurants, hotels and cars were scarce; historic buildings were in a state of decay.

And the Berlin Wall was heavily guarded.

I was filled with sadness.

Colleen kept asking, "How can people live like this?"

When we boarded the train for Prague, we found our sleeping car had only three beds. I suggested we double up; I didn't want my family to be separated. The conductor decided otherwise and sent Patrick promptly off to find a seat in a third-class car.

Several times throughout the night, our passports and visas were thoroughly examined; our pictures were compared to our faces by authorities who shined flashlights into our eyes.

We arrived in Prague in the early morning, relieved to meet up with Patrick.

He had spent the night comparing lifestyles and playing cards with some young East German men. They were impressed that Patrick had a driver's license and that he wore his Chicago Bears hat backward.

Prague was beautiful. It had more energy than East Berlin, but it was communist and life didn't look easy.

A few months after our trip, East Germans began fleeing their homeland. Then restrictions on their travel were lifted.

DECEMBER

At first, I thought I would want out, too. Then reality hit. As difficult as life was in East Germany, it was home to its people.

The answer was the wall - it had to crumble. When it did, there was dancing in the streets. This jubilation was followed by dramatic political reforms in Czechoslovakia.

Our trip and the subsequent political events in Eastern Europe have made me realize that there always will be struggle, injustice, pain and suffering in the world.

But if we strive to improve from within and rise to the occasion, as the Czechs did in Prague, our search for truth and beauty will keep us on the trail blazed at the birth of Christ.

The spirit of Christmas brings joy to the world. This year, it is taking a step closer in the direction of peace on earth and good will toward men.

December 25, 1989

* * * *

Family of Believers
. . . Behold the Spirit of Christmas

Christmas Eve, 1991.

Conversations around our house lately have been about the existence of Santa Claus.

When you think about it, Santa Claus is not a very plausible concept, especially the part about him crisscrossing the country with a team of flying reindeer and sliding down chimneys. That chimney part worried me as a child.

When I was growing up, we always had a fire in the fireplace on winter evenings. I would ask my Dad not to light a fire on Christmas Eve so Santa wouldn't get scorched. Dad would tell me it was OK because Santa was like magic and a fire wouldn't bother him. That made sense to me.

My little guys rationalize Santa's inconsistencies with blind faith. After all, love is blind and Santa certainly is someone who inspires love.

My sons wonder why some of their friends don't believe in Santa Claus. I think my sons have come to the conclusion that these nonbelievers are going to be sorry.

My children aren't taking any chances. They are not doubting Santa's existence. They want Santa to believe in them, too.

Mike asked if we could buy film for the camera. If it snows, he wants to take pictures of the tracks Santa's reindeer leave on the roof.

Johnny suggested setting up the video camera to record everything that happened after he went to bed. Then he reconsidered. "There's probably not a videotape long enough to last the whole night," he said.

My children are believers. So is my husband. So am I.

I've always been a believer. Once I saw the real Santa Claus on Christmas Eve. Honest. I was 8 years old. I was in the bedroom I shared with my sisters. We were supposed to be asleep, but we were too excited.

Suddenly, my brother, John, who was the oldest, ran into our room and said, "You better get to sleep. Santa's coming. He won't stop at our house if you are still awake, and I just heard him. He's over at the Sorensens' house."

We all ran to the window, and a couple of seconds later I saw Santa and his reindeer fly across our front lawn. And just as quickly, I jumped back into bed and went to sleep.

It was very exciting. It is something that happens only on a magical night such as this.

It's Christmas Eve. Everything looks different, somehow. The stoplights and the gas stations on the corner, and the parks and the street in front of our house all look different. These places aren't even decorated for Christmas, yet they have a special look.

The Christ Child envisioned a peaceful world filled with joy, kindness and unconditional love. Sometimes we depart from Jesus' path for us. Believing in Santa Claus is like believing in ourselves. To believe, we have to forget skepticism and cynicism and have dreams of hope, love and sharing.

That's the spirit of Christmas as Jesus intended.

December 24, 1991

* * * *

Counting Blessings at Christmastime

Six-year-old Matt was following me around the house asking questions about bad luck. I was replying to his queries - "How do you get bad luck?" and "What is bad luck?" - with half-attentive responses. I was preoccupied with hanging some Christmas garland.

Finally he said, "Do you wonder why I'm asking about bad luck?"

I hadn't really wondered, but now that he asked me I was quite interested. I stopped what I was doing and said, "Why are you asking about bad luck?"

"I think I'm going to have some bad luck," Matt told me. "I walked under a ladder (which was set up in the house to decorate the Christmas tree). That's why I'm carrying around these." He showed me two four-leaf clover paperweights he had in the pocket of his sweat pants.

I told him he probably wouldn't have bad luck just from walking under a ladder. That was just a superstition and he shouldn't worry about it, I said. But then I told him it wouldn't hurt to carry the four-leaf clovers just in case.

Of course, Matt doesn't understand about superstitions and neither do I. Even though I don't really believe in superstitions I'm also afraid not to. I've never wanted to tempt fate.

For example, I've always wondered why I am so lucky. I don't mean at cards or at the races but lucky in life. But I'm too superstitious to try to figure it out.

Happiness and good fortune are a powerful burden to carry. As opposed to someone who doesn't have any good things in life and therefore nothing to lose, I have so much and also so much to lose. I, of course, prefer the latter set of circumstances, but it is frightening.

At the Christmas season it is appropriate to extend wishes to others that only good things come to them. It also is a time to do something to make good things come to others who need our help. There are so many people who need more than a four-leaf clover paperweight to ward off bad luck.

The greatest joy in life is my family and friends. The happiness they give me each day fills my heart in a way I'm sure nothing else could ever begin to do.

I love my children so intensely and so unconditionally that I sometime surprise myself at my ability to do so. It is a fulfilling and joyous sensation that can be described only as a Blessing.

So when I think of God giving us Jesus, His Son I am in awe of the magnitude of that gift. It was a gift of the greatest love to others.

The Christmas season is a time for giving of gifts of many types. We have a lot of loot stashed around our house to be put under the tree on Christmas Eve. Every year I think we overdo it. but I guess that is part of the season. It is fun to delight others with presents. I think it is also fun to be the recipient of a few gifts. The other part of Christmas is remembering the spiritual gifts we have been given and to spread them all around the place.

One of my favorite songs is sung during the Liturgy of the Eucharist during the Mass. The congregation joins in singing what we Catholics call the "Holy, Holy, Holy." The last line is "Blessed is he who comes in the name of the Lord. Hosanna in the highest." To me that means that if we do all in the name of the Lord the spirit of Christmas will be forever with us.

My second favorite song is one Matt learned two years ago at preschool: "It Must be Santa Claus."

December 22, 1992

* * * *

HOPE FOR THE BEST ALWAYS

the end